SCOTTISH NATIONALIST PARTIES

Books LLC®, Reference Series, Memphis, USA, 2011. www.booksllc.net. Copyright: http://creativecommons.org/licenses/by-sa/3.0/deed.en

Table of Contents

Scottish National Party
55 Group 1
79 Group 2
A Constitution for a Free Scotland 3
Campaign for Nationalism in Scotland 5
Choosing Scotland's Future 5
Federation of Student Nationalists 5
Glasgow Govan by-election, 1988 6
Glasgow University Scottish Nationalist Association 6
Henry Cunison Rankin 6
History of the Scottish National Party 7
It's Scotland's oil 11
Labour Party of Scotland 12
Moray by-election, 2006 13
National Conversation 13
Orkney and Shetland Movement 14
Radio Free Scotland 14
Referendum (Scotland) Bill, 2010 15
SNP Trade Union Group 18
SNP fundamentalist 19
SNP gradualist 19
Scots National League 19
Scots Wha Hae 19
Scottish Labour Party (1976) 20
Scottish National Party 20
Scottish Party 23
Scottish Socialist Party (1987) 23
The Scots Independent 23
Young Scots for Independence 23

Scottish nationalist parties
Free Scotland Party 24
Scottish Enterprise Party 24
Scottish Jacobite Party 25
Scottish Republican Socialist Party .. 26
Scottish Socialist Party 26

Introduction

Purchase of this book entitles you to a free trial membership in the publisher's book club at www.booksllc.net. (Time limited offer.) Simply enter the barcode number from the back cover onto the membership form. The book club entitles you to select from hundreds of thousands of books at no additional charge. You can also download a digital copy of this and related books to read on the go. Simply enter the title or subject onto the search form to find them.

Each chapter in this book ends with a URL to a hyperlinked online version. Type the URL exactly as it appears. If you change the URL's capitalization it won't work. Use the online version to access related pages, websites, footnotes, tables, color photos, updates. Click the version history tab to see the chapter's contributors. Click the edit link to suggest changes.

A large and diverse editor base collaboratively wrote the book, not a single author. After a long process of discussion and debate, the chapters gradually took on a neutral point of view reached through consensus. Additional editors expanded and contributed to chapters striving to achieve balance and comprehensive coverage. This reduced the regional or cultural bias found in many other books and provided access and breadth on subject matter otherwise little documented.

55 Group

The **55 Group** were an internal body within the Scottish National Party (SNP) formed in 1955 (hence the name of the group).

This grouping started an organised campaign of internal dissent. This group was formed mainly of younger SNP members frustrated at the lack of electoral progress of the party in this period. There was also overt tones of anti-English sentiment amongst this grouping, epitomised by the publication of a leaflet *The English: Are They Human?*.

This anti-English streak proved too much to bear for the SNP leadership and the 55 Group were expelled.

Some of their members went on to form a new political party, the National Party of Scotland (NPS) (not to be confused with the earlier NPS which merged with the Scottish Party in 1934 to form the SNP). This split in the SNP proved to be minor and involved only a few members, mainly located in the city of Edinburgh, and the new NPS made no impact whatsoever in the long-run.

The 55 Group are not the only organisation to have been proscribed by the SNP. In the early 1980s the 79 Group (like the 55 Group, named after the year they were formed, but unlike the 55 Group not an anti-English body, but a radical socialist organisation) and Siol nan Gaidheal were banned, and in more recent times they have banned their members from joining the Scottish Republican Socialist Movement.

Source (edited): "http://en.wikipedia.org/wiki/55_Group"

79 Group

The **79 Group** was an internal faction within the Scottish National Party (SNP), named after the fact that it was formed in 1979. The group sought to persuade the SNP to take an active left-wing stance, arguing that it would win more support, and were highly critical of the established SNP leaders. Although it had a tiny membership, the group caused sufficient disquiet that they were expelled from the SNP in 1982, although its members were subsequently readmitted and many attained senior positions in the Scottish Government after 2007; First Minister Alex Salmond was a leading member of the group.

Background

The idea for the 79 Group came from Roseanna Cunningham, then assistant research officer for the SNP, and her brother Chris, during the devolution referendum in early 1979. Although a majority of those voting backed devolution in the referendum, the vote was close and crucially the Yes votes did not reach the 40% threshold set by Parliament. At the SNP national council meeting a few days after the result of the referendum, Margo MacDonald argued that because working-class Scots had supported devolution and middle-class Scots had opposed, the SNP should aim to build its support among the working-class.

A group of eight SNP members who shared this opinion met on 10 March 1979. Before they could meet again, the SNP lost nine of its 11 seats in the 1979 general election; the poor result prompted a period of internal questioning by many SNP members about the direction the party should take. More than 30 attended a second meeting at the Belford Hotel in Edinburgh on 31 May which agreed to set up an "Interim Committee for Political Discussion". This interim committee later became the 79 Group.

Formation

The founders decided to establish their group on a formal footing, with membership cards and elected officers. Three spokespeople were appointed, including Margo MacDonald and Alex Salmond. Stephen Maxwell became the group's principal political theorist. The group was formed as a left wing organisation committed to the establishment of a "socialist and republican Scotland". They began producing campaign material in support of their policies, and standing for internal SNP posts. The established SNP wing, now dubbed "traditionalists", disliked the party appearing ideological. Winifred Ewing eventually formed the 'Campaign for Nationalism in Scotland' as a second internal SNP group to oppose the 79 Group.

Many SNP activists became attracted to the 79 Group, seeing it as a debating forum to discuss the SNP's future, but most left quickly when not attracted by the ideology driving the group. At the 1979 SNP conference, 79 Group candidates were heavily defeated by those in the SNP who put achieving independence over all other policy considerations.

Advances

In 1980, the former Labour MP and founder of the Scottish Labour Party, Jim Sillars, joined the SNP along with some other SLP members. Given the SLP's stance on the left, Sillars was naturally in line with the 79 Group's policy and immediately joined it too. Although no members of the 79 Group were elected to the SNP National executive at the 1980 conference less than a month after Sillars joined, at the 1981 SNP conference, five were.

Scottish Resistance

A passionate appeal by Stephen Maxwell failed to get a motion critical of private industry passed at the 1981 conference, but conference did vote by a big majority for a motion calling for "a real Scottish resistance" including "political strikes and civil disobedience on a mass scale" after a speech by Sillars. The new policy, dubbed "Scottish Resistance", was unveiled in September 1981 with a logo consisting of figures with raised clenched fists.

Sillars, who was elected as the SNP's Executive Vice-Chairman for Policy, was put in charge of the campaign with the details planned by the Demonstrations Committee. He led the campaign on 16 October 1981 by breaking in, with five other 79 Group members, to the Royal High School in Edinburgh which had been converted to be the Scottish Assembly. The intention had been to symbolically read out a declaration on what the Scottish Assembly would have done to counter unemployment, but the participants were arrested before they had the chance, and a planned later mass demonstration was cancelled. Sillars was later fined for wilful damage by breaking a window to get in. Many in the SNP were uncomfortable with this sort of action; three senior members were quoted in *The Scotsman* opposing the occupation.

Decline of the 79 Group

Early in 1982, Sinn Féin wrote inviting a 79 Group speaker to its ardfheis (conference). With IRA violence ongoing, Sinn Féin were considered unacceptable by most of public opinion. Alex Salmond moved to reject the request and won, but minutes of the meeting were leaked to the press, linking the two groups. Soon after, the 1982 conference of the SNP voted to ditch "Scottish Resistance", despite a strong speech by Salmond claiming that to do so was to adopt "a defeatist and cringing mentality". Many non-79 Group members felt that the civil disobedience campaign had collapsed in farce.

The SNP leadership under Gordon Wilson finally decided that the group's activity must be stopped. At the 1982 SNP conference in Ayr, Wilson threatened to resign unless the conference passed a motion to proscribe all organised political groupings within the party (the motion covered Winifred Ewing's Campaign for Nationalism in Scotland as well). He won what was described as a Pyrrhic victory by 308 to 188. However the 79 Group's members mostly retained their offices within the party.

Expulsions

After the conference resolution, the 79 Group decided to agree to disband, but rather than going away, the Group formed an interim committee to create the "79 Group Socialist Society" outside the party. The interim committee was the same as the executive of the 79 Group. The National Executive declared that membership of this committee was incompatible with that of the SNP.

Armed with the conference mandate, the leadership then moved to expel the leading 79 Group members. Alex Salmond, Kenny MacAskill, Stephen Maxwell, and others were expelled; Roseanna Cunningham was not, on the grounds that she was not a member of the interim committee. Margo MacDonald was not expelled but resigned from the SNP in protest. Other members of the 79 Group in party offices were left alone; when the expelled members appealed against their expulsion, the committee hearing the appeal included 79 Group member Stewart Stevenson.

A Scottish Socialist Society was formed, open to non-SNP members; among those who joined were Susan Deacon and Sarah Boyack, who later became Labour MSPs. However the society was short-lived.

The appeals were narrowly rejected when the SNP National Council debated the report of the Appeals Committee. However, the substantial support for those expelled and the minority report submitted by Stewart Stevenson persuaded National Council to allow their re-admission to the SNP. Once back in the party many would go on to high office in the SNP.

Source (edited): "http://en.wikipedia.org/wiki/79_Group"

A Constitution for a Free Scotland

In September 2002, the Scottish National Party (SNP) published a document, entitled **"A Constitution for a Free Scotland"**, which details their policy for the Constitution of a future independent Scotland. This Constitution, which would come into effect following Scotland's transition to independence, would set out the rights of citizens of an independent Scotland, and define the powers and responsibilities of government and parliament.

Historical background

The 2002 paper represents the culmination of many years' work. The essential elements of the Constitutional Policy were first adopted at the SNP's National Conference in 1977. The original drafting committee was convened by the late Dr Robert McIntyre, assisted by Professor Neil MacCormick, Dr Allan Macartney, Peter Chiene, Kenneth Fee, Isobel Lindsay and Barbara Park. The spirit of the original proposal has been retained in subsequent revisions, including a substantial review in 1990–1991.

Aims and principles

The SNP Draft Constitution declares itself to be necessary "to protect the rights of every Scottish citizen and to place restrictions on what politicians can and can't do". The draft "envisages an inclusive Scotland that embraces its geographic and cultural diversity, where its citizens are free from discrimination on any grounds in the exercise of their constitutional rights". The intention is to "give voice to the Scottish people and provide the means for us to take control of the decisions affecting our lives".

Article One: Constitution and People

Article One, entitled "Constitution and People" sets out some of the foundations of the Scottish State, including:

(1) The right of the people of Scotland to self-determination and national sovereignty.

(2) A declaration of Scotland's territorial claims to the mainland and islands of Scotland, and to Scotland's offshore (oil and gas) resources.

(3) A declaration of constitutional supremacy: the Constitution is the supreme law and any other legislation which is incompatible with the Constitution will therefore be null and void.

(4) An inclusive definition of citizenship, with reserved rights of residency for non-citizens resident in Scotland at the time of independence. Voting is from age 16.

Note that there is no preamble or declaration of principles, and no mention of Scotland's flag, anthem, or capital.

Article Two: Head of State and Executive

Article Two sets out the arrangement for the Head of State and the Executive:

(1) The Queen (Elizabeth II) would be retained as Head of State, with the title of "Queen of Scots". The Union of 1603 – a personal union between the Scots Crown and that of England – would thereby be maintained, even though the Union of 1707 – a governmental union of two States and two Parliaments – would be dissolved.

(2) The Constitution for Scotland states that the monarch would hold title under the law of Scotland, so presumably the Parliament of Scotland could, at some future time, alter the law of succession in such a way that this personal union is dissolved. A Scottish Parliament would also be able, if it so desired at some future time, to remove the religious proscriptions which ban Roman Catholics from inheriting the Crown under the Act of Settlement.

(3) Executive powers are vested in the Head of State, who is expected and required to act on the advice of the Prime Minister and Ministers. The Prime Minister is to be elected by Parliament, and Ministers are to be confirmed by Parliament. The government as a whole is accountable to Parliament by means of a motion of confidence, in accordance with the rules of the parliamentary system.

(4) When the Queen is not present in Scotland, the elected Presiding Officer (i.e. Speaker) of Parliament would act

as Head of State.

The SNP is committed to holding a referendum on the future of the monarchy within the first term of a post-independence Parliament, but no explicit provision for this is made in the proposed Constitution.

Article Three: The Legislature

Article Three makes provision for a Parliament of Scotland, which will possess legislative (law making) power, as well as being responsible for debating policies and holding the Executive to account.

The Constitution makes a number of breaks from British constitutional practice which were seen as radical in the 1970s but are, according to the SNP's Policy Paper, now accepted as part of Scottish political life:

(1) The Parliament of Scotland will be unicameral, in keeping with the tradition of the old Scottish Parliament before 1707 and that of the Devolved Scottish Parliament today.

(2) The Parliament will be elected by proportional representation. The SNP favours the Single Transferable Vote system, but the exact electoral system used will be determined by ordinary legislation.

(3) Parliament elected for four-year fixed terms. Early dissolution is permitted only if a government enjoying parliamentary support cannot be formed: the Prime Minister cannot dissolve Parliament at will. Parliament may also extend its term of office, in times of war, for up to one year.

(4) To compensate for the lack of a second chamber, a minority veto procedure (whereby two-fifths of the members of Parliament can delay a bill for up to a year, subject to the right of the majority to refer the bill to the people in a referendum) is included. This is intended to prevent rash legislation by a Parliamentary majority.

(5) A stronger committee system will also be instituted, with pre-legislative scrutiny of legislation in parliamentary committees, although the Constitution is sparse on detail.

(6) Parliament would have control over declarations of war and the ratification of treaties. Treaties which amend the Constitution (e.g. treaties of European integration) must be passed by a three-fifths majority in Parliament and ratified by a national referendum.

Article Four: Local Government

Article Four recognises and guarantees the independence of elected local Councils, which are also to be elected by proportional representation. The Islands authorities (Orkney, Shetland and the Western Isles) also have certain guaranteed privileges which may not be removed by ordinary legislation.

Note: the constitutionally guaranteed status of local Councils was not included in the 1977 document, but has been included in the 2002 version.

Article Five: The Judiciary

The Constitution recognises the independence of the judiciary:

(1) Judges are to be appointed by the Head of State on the advice of an independent appointments commission, consisting of the Lord Advocate, the Presiding Officer of Parliament, a Senator of the College of Justice and two impartial members elected by Parliament.

(2) Judges may only be removed from office, for misconduct, by a two-thirds majority vote of Parliament.

Article Six: Fundamental Rights and Liberties

The Constitution entrenches a number of fundamental rights and liberties, including freedom of speech, religion, assembly, movement, privacy, fair trial, due process etc. These are based on the European Convention on Human Rights.

Social and economic rights, such as entitlements to public housing, unemployment benefit, pensions, public healthcare, and education, are included, but there is no protection for trial by jury and no rule preventing double jeopardy.

The rights and liberties guaranteed in the Constitution may be waived during a State of Emergency. A State of Emergency must be approved by a three-fifths majority of the members of Parliament within two weeks, and may continue for up to three months, after which it must be renewed by Parliament.

Article Seven: Amendments

The Constitution may be amended by a three-fifths majority vote of Parliament, subject to approval by a majority of the people in a referendum.

Other noteworthy features

(1) The SNP draft Constitution is noticeably shorter than most modern (post-1945 and post-1989) European Constitutions, at around 6000 words.

(2) The relationships between the Executive and the Parliament are not clearly defined, particularly with regard to the election of a Prime Minister and the procedure for votes of confidence. This leaves scope for the regulation of these matters by law, standing orders of Parliament, or, in the absence of such provision, by existing parliamentary custom.

(3) In contrast to contempary European practice, the SNP's Constitution for Scotland does not clearly distinguish between the respective roles of the Head of State and the Executive (compare with the Constitutions of Spain or Sweden, where such a distinction is explicitly made).

(4) The Constitution does specify the size of Parliament, only that it must be at least four times the size of the Executive (the number of Ministers is limited to one-fifth of the members of Parliament).

(5) The qualifications for membership of Parliament, and any incompatibilities between membership of Parliament and other public offices, are unspecified. These matters are subject to determination by Parliament, in accordance with the usual legislative process.

(6) There is no mention in the Constitution for an Auditor-General or an Ombudsman, although both institutions currently exist in Scotland under Statute law. There is provision for Freedom of Information, but no reference to the Scottish Information Commissioner.

Source (edited): "http://en.wikipedia.org/wiki/A_Constitution_for_a_Free

Campaign for Nationalism in Scotland

The **Campaign for Nationalism in Scotland** was an internal grouping within the Scottish National Party (SNP) that formed in response to the efforts of the 79 Group within the party. The 79 Group was another internal grouping within the SNP that was attempting to turn the party into an expressly socialist party. The Campaign for Nationalism in Scotland formed itself to try and ensure that the SNP avoided traditional debates of left and right, arguing that the cause of Scottish independence transcended such arguments. It had the support of prominent traditionalists inside the party such as Winnie Ewing who had been a Member of Parliament in the 1960s and was by this stage a Member of the European Parliament.

SNP leader Gordon Wilson was determined to end factionalism inside the SNP, and at the party conference of 1982 internal groupings were banned. This was largely a reaction to the growth of the 79 Group who faded in significance after this decision was taken. After the 79 Group fell apart the Campaign for Nationalism in Scotland did likewise (however, many of the members of the 79 group were readmitted, and indeed came to lead the party).

Source (edited): "http://en.wikipedia.org/wiki/Campaign_for_Nationalism_in_Scotland"

Choosing Scotland's Future

Choosing Scotland's Future is a white paper published on 14 August 2007, by the Scottish Government.

As a tagline, it uses Parnell's:

No man has a right to fix the boundary of the march of a nation; no man has a right to say to his country, "Thus far shalt thou go and no further".

Source (edited): "http://en.wikipedia.org/wiki/Choosing_Scotland%27s_Future"

Federation of Student Nationalists

The **Federation of Student Nationalists** (FSN) (sometimes termed **SNP Students**) is the student wing of the Scottish National Party (SNP), representing students in Scottish higher education. It was formed in the 1960s when various student organisations supportive of Scottish independence and the Scottish National Party in particular decided to join forces into a new constituent body.

It is not to be confused with Young Scots for Independence, which is the youth wing of the SNP - the FSN is for those in higher education, and membership is not restricted by age.

The FSN is an autonomous body from the SNP and as such can devise its own policies, publicity and campaigns. Unlike the SNP it is expressly republican, and has in the past exhibited socialist sentiments.

History

Key figures in the formation of the FSN were Neil MacCormick and Allan MacCartney who would both later become SNP members of the European Parliament.

It has played an active part in the affairs of the SNP and is represented on the party's National Executive Committee, in the past with a representative position shared with the Young Scots for Independence, but now each organisation has its own representative. The FSN can send delegates to the SNP Annual National Conference and meetings of its National Council.

In the 2000 SNP Leadership campaign the FSN supported Alex Neil who lost to John Swinney. In the two subsequent leadership campaigns the organisation did not officially endorse any candidate.

It has informal links with Cymru X, the youth wing of Plaid Cymru.

In September 2008 FSN caused controversy by opposing the SNP-led Scottish Government's proposal to raise the minimum purchase age for alcohol in off-sales from 18 to 21.

Current office holders

- National Convener: Gail Lythgoe, Edinburgh University Scottish Nationalist Association (EUSNA).
- Vice Convener: Fiona Gardner, Edinburgh University Scottish Nationalist Association (EUSNA).
- Secretary: Gary Cocker, Dundee University Student Nationalist Association (DUSNA).
- Organiser: Andrew Philbin MVP, Stirling University Scottish Nationalist Association (SUSNA).
- Treasurer: Fiona Gardner, Edinburgh University Student Nationalist Association (EUSNA).
- IT Officer: Cevin, Stirling University Scottish Nationalist Association (SUSNA).
- Publicity Officer: Michael Hutchison, Aberdeen University Scottish Nationalist Association (AUSNA).
- Ordinary Executive Members: Euan Campbell, Edinburgh University Student Nationalist Association (EUSNA), Angus MacLeod

Glasgow Govan by-election, 1988

The **Glasgow Govan by-election**, in the British House of Commons constituency of Glasgow Govan, Scotland, was held on 10 November 1988. It was caused by the resignation of Bruce Millan as Member of Parliament for the constituency.

The result was a major upset for the Labour Party, with former Labour MP Jim Sillars winning the seat for the Scottish National Party with a majority of 3,554.

Source (edited): "http://en.wikipedia.org/wiki/Glasgow_Govan_by-election,_1988"

Glasgow University Scottish Nationalist Association

The **Glasgow University Scottish Nationalist Association** (**GUSNA**) is a student organisation formed in 1927 at the University of Glasgow which supports Scottish independence.

GUSNA is important historically as it predated many pro-independence organisations including the Scottish National Party itself. It is the forerunner of the National Party of Scotland (NPS), which it played a key role in forming, which is itself a forerunner of the modern Scottish National Party.

History

One prime mover in the formation of GUSNA was John MacCormick who had previously been involved in the Glasgow University Labour Club.

GUSNA was thrown into prominence in the early 1950s when a group of its members (including Ian Hamilton who would later become a well known Queen's Counsel) took the Stone of Destiny from Westminster Abbey on Christmas Day 1950. This caused a huge scandal amongst the British establishment and it wasn't until April 1951 that the stone was found by the authorities.

GUSNA has, almost since its inception, tried to play an active part in the life of Glasgow University with its members regularly being involved in the Students' Representative Council as well as regularly nominating candidates for the election of the Rectorship of the university. Notable GUSNA Rectorial candidates of the past have included Robert Cunninghame-Graham and John MacCormick (who with Ian Hamilton as his campaign manager was successful in being elected). More recent candidates have been Pat Kane, Dorothy-Grace Elder, Ian Hamilton and the noted writer and artist Alasdair Gray. GUSNA is a constituent member of the SNP Student Wing, the Federation of Student Nationalists (FSN) and played a leading role in the FSN's formation in the 1960s.

Prominent former members of GUSNA have included Winnie Ewing and Neil MacCormick MEP (son of John MacCormick). The current president is Iain Wallace.

Source (edited): "http://en.wikipedia.org/wiki/Glasgow_University_Scottish_Nationalist_Association"

Henry Cunison Rankin

Henry Cunison Rankin (1932–2010) was a Scottish chartered accountant who served as treasurer to the Scottish National Party and as National Chairman of the Saltire Society.

Henry Cunison Deans Rankin was born at Hamilton, Scotland, on 14 October 1932 and was educated at the former Hamilton Academy and the University of Glasgow, graduating MA and LLB in 1958.

Joining the tax department of the Glasgow firm of Arthur Young McLelland Moores and Company in 1967, Rankin subsequently moved in 1970 to the Edinburgh firm of chartered accountants, Graham Smart and Annan, becoming tax manager. In 1973 Rankin was appointed a lecturer on taxation at the Institute of Chartered Accountants of Scotland and in 1982 appointed the Institute's director of student education. Rankin also wrote a classic textbook *Corporation Tax for Students* used by accountancy students across the U.K.

Rankin stood unsuccessfully on the Scottish National Party (SNP) ticket as a parliamentary candidate for the Lanark constituency in 1966 and 1970, and for the North Angus and Mearns constituency in 1974. He served as SNP national treasurer from 1965–66, and as a member of its National Executive Committee from 1966–68.

In June 2007 Rankin was appointed National Chairman of the Saltire Society. For eleven years since its inception, Rankin also served as treasurer and secretary of the Cantilena Music Festival, held twice a year on the Isle of Islay, Scotland.

Henry Cunison Rankin died at Dunfermline on 4 January 2010.

Source (edited): "http://en.wikipedia.org/wiki/Henry_Cunison_Rankin"

History of the Scottish National Party

In Scotland, the **Scottish National Party** (SNP) is a centre-left political party which campaigns for Scottish independence. It currently holds power in Scotland with its leader Alex Salmond as First Minister of Scotland, following the outcome of the 2007 Scottish General Election.

Early years

The party was founded on 20 April 1934 as the result of a merger between the National Party of Scotland (NPS) and the Scottish Party. The merger was the brainchild of leading NPS figure John MacCormick who desired unity for the nationalist movement in Scotland, and upon learning of the Scottish Party's emergence moved to secure it.

Initially, the SNP did not support all-out independence for Scotland, but rather the establishment of a devolved Scottish Assembly, within the United Kingdom. This became the party's initial position on the constitutional status of Scotland as a result of a compromise between the NPS, who did support independence, and the Scottish Party who were devolutionists. John MacCormick wanted a merger between the two parties and knew that it would only be through the support of devolution rather than independence that the Scottish Party would be persuaded to merge. However, the SNP quickly reverted to the NPS stance of supporting full independence for Scotland.

Professor Douglas Young, was the leader of the Scottish National Party from 1942 to 1945. Young fought for the Scottish people to refuse conscription and his activities were popularly vilified as undermining the British war effort against the Nazis. Young was imprisoned for refusing to be conscripted.

John McCormick left the party in 1942, owing to his failure to change the party's policy from supporting all out independence to Home Rule at that year's SNP conference in Glasgow. McCormick went on to form the Scottish Covenant Association, a non-partisan political organisation campaigning for the establishment of a devolved Scottish Assembly. This Covenant in itself proved politically challenging for the SNP, as it stole their nationalist platform. It also deprived the party of many members who left with MacCormick.

Professor Douglas Young, became the leader of the Scottish National Party from 1942 to 1945. Young fought for Scottish people to refuse conscription in the British war effort against the Nazis. Young was imprisoned for refusing to be conscripted.

The Covenant managed to get over 2 million signatures to a petition demanding Home Rule for Scotland in the late 1940s and early 1950s, and secured support from across the parties, but it eventually faded as a political force.

The SNP's early years were characterised by a lack of electoral progress and it wasn't until 1945 that the SNP's first member was elected to the UK parliament at Westminster. The party's first MP was Robert McIntyre who won a by-election for the Motherwell constituency. However he lost the seat in the general election of that year.

McIntyre's brief spell did not particularly galvanise the SNP. The 1950s were characterised by low levels of support, and this made it difficult for the party to advance. Indeed, in most general elections they were unable to put up more than a handful of candidates.

A split occurred in the SNP in 1955 (although not as large as that of 1942) when a grouping styled the 55 Group started an organised campaign of internal dissent. This group was formed mainly of younger SNP members frustrated at the lack of progress of the party. This split proved to be minor and involved only a few members, mainly located in the city of Edinburgh, and the new National Party of Scotland made no impact whatsoever in the long-run.

Party Growth in the 1960s

Despite the poor record the SNP had in the 1950s by the 1960s they were beginning to make more impact. William Wolfe, who would become party leader in the 1970s performed very well at the 1962 West Lothian by-election, which Tam Dalyell won for Labour. The party began to grow quickly in the 1960s with a rapid growth in the number of recognised branches. For example, in 1966 alone the SNP National Executive recognised 113 new branches of the party. 1967 was the year that the party signalled they could begin to make an impact electorally. The party polled very well at the Pollok by-election, winning some 28% of the votes cast in a constituency where they had never stood before. This signalled the beginning of an upward electoral trend for the SNP.

Later that year that the SNP scored an even greater electoral success, projecting them into the political limelight. Winnie Ewing won the Hamilton constituency in a by-election in 1967 with the help of national organizer John McAteer. Consequently, the SNP began to make a serious impact on the political scene. Ewing famously said on the night of her by-election victory, 'stop the world, Scotland wants to get on', and this spirit seemed to be embraced by many Scots. Her victory propelled the party into the popular conscience and many new members joined as a result.

A novel feature of the 1967 SNP Annual Conference was that the party leader Arthur Donaldson was challenged for the convenorship of the party. His challenger was Douglas Drysdale who was critical of the way Donaldson was leading the SNP. Donaldson overwhelmingly defeated Drysdale to retain his position.

In local elections the SNP were beginning to show they could compete also. In the 1967 Local Council elections, the SNP secured over 200,000 votes across the country making 27 gains in the burgh elections, and 42 in the counties. They managed to take control of Stirling council where former party leader Robert McIntyre became Provost. The SNP then went onto secure the largest share of the Scottish vote of any of the parties contesting the 1968 Local Council elections, winning some

40% of the vote.

Ewing's by-election victory and this improved electoral performance in the local elections helped to provoke the then UK Labour Government to establish the Kilbrandon Commission to set up the blue-print for the establishment of a devolved Scottish Assembly. It also prompted Edward Heath's announcement at the Conservative Perth Conference in 1968 that if he became Prime Minister he would establish a Scottish Assembly.

Scotland's unionist politicians were becoming increasingly worried at the growth of the SNP. The Labour Party in particular had cause for alarm as Scotland provided so much of their support base, and the SNP were now picking up support in their very heartlands.

At the 1969 party conference, Billy Wolfe was elected SNP leader in place of Arthur Donaldson.

Highpoint in the 1970s

However, at the 1970 General Election, the SNP did not make major advances. Ewing lost her Hamilton seat and the only consolation for the SNP was the capture of the Western Isles with Donald Stewart becoming their sole Westminster representative. Thereafter though the 1970s was a period of sustained growth for the SNP. They followed the pattern of the 1960s with a number of strong showings in individual by-elections.

There was a minor setback in the early 1970s when a small number of party members in Dundee left to form a Labour Party of Scotland. This new party contested the Dundee East by-election of 1973, and the number of votes they captured was more than the "official" Labour candidates margin of victory over the SNP candidate, Gordon Wilson. However, in the long-run this new party folded, and most of its members returned to the SNP.

They were bolstered by their capture of the Glasgow Govan seat with Margo MacDonald as their candidate from the Labour Party in a by-election in 1973. This again signalled to Labour that the SNP posed an electoral threat to them and in the February 1974 General Election they returned 7 MPs. The failure of the Labour Party to secure an overall majority prompted them to quickly return to the polls to secure such and in the October 1974 General Election the SNP performed even better than they had done earlier in the year, winning 11 MPs and managing to get over 30% of the vote across Scotland. The main driving force behind the growth of the SNP in the 1970s was the discovery of oil in the North Sea off the coast of Scotland. The SNP ran a hugely successful *It's Scotland's oil* campaign, emphasising the way in which they believed the discovery of oil could benefit all of Scotland's citizens.

Former SNP leader Billy Wolfe has argued that along with this campaign, the SNP was aided by their support for the workers in the Upper Clyde Shipbuilders Work-in, being led by Jimmy Reid, as well as supporting the workers at the Scottish Daily Express when they attempted to run the paper themselves and other such campaigns.

The SNP continued to ride high in the opinion polls throughout the 1970s, and many members are convinced that if the Liberals, led by David Steel hadn't maintained the Labour Government of the time in power, the SNP might have made further electoral gains in the resulting general election. It did well at the local elections of 1977, making 98 net gains and leaving half of Scotland under hung councils. However 1978 saw a Labour revival at the expense of the SNP, at three by-elections (Glasgow Garscadden, Hamilton and Berwick and East Lothian) and the local elections. The general election did not come till 1979, by which time the party's support had dwindled.

In 1979, the SNP Parliamentary Group voted against the Labour Government in a Vote of No Confidence, causing the dissolution of the government and subsequent election. The then Labour Prime Minister, James Callaghan famously described this decision by the SNP as that of, 'turkeys voting for Christmas'. This statement would prove true, as the no-confidence vote by the SNP led to the loss of their Westminster seats and the dawn of Margaret Thatcher.

Interference by the UK Government

The party was accused of being paranoid when it claimed that it was being spied upon by government agents. The SNP's paranoia was justified when leaked government files proved that the government had in fact spied on the SNP. During the 1970s, the British government used both police and agents placed within trade unions to limit the growth of the SNP the best it could. The Labour Party, which controlled the government in this time, has drawn consistent Scottish support since Labour's founding had seen the SNP become much more than a protest vote in the '70s. It is alleged that government interference is part of what helped bring about the collapse in support for the party in 1979. Labour continues to ridicule the SNP for their claims of government interference. "The SNP appears totally paranoid. All the evidence shows they are absolutely no threat whatsoever to the British state," said a Labour spokesperson in response to the SNP's complaints. Despite these words, the Labour government has had several files on the SNP sealed for fifty years, citing reasons of national security.

Factionalism after 1979

The party went into a period of decline after the failure to secure a devolved Scottish Assembly in 1979 and its poor performance in the general election of that year. A period of internal strife followed, culminating in the proscription of two internal groups, Siol nan Gaidheal and the left-wing 79 Group. However, several 79 Group members would later return to prominence in the party, including Alex Salmond who would later lead the party. It proved too much for Margo MacDonald though, who was defeated by Douglas Henderson for the position of party deputy leader at the 1979 party conference, and left the SNP, angry at the treatment of the left wing of the party, although she would later return to the party and be elected as an MSP.

There was also another internal grouping formed within the party, primarily as a response to the growth of the 79 Group entitled the Campaign for Nationalism in Scotland, with the support of traditionalists such as Winnie Ewing. This group sought to ensure that the primary objective of the SNP was campaigning for independence regardless of any traditional left-right ideology, and if it had been successful would have undone the work of figures such as Billy Wolfe moving the SNP to become a clearly defined social-democratic party in the 1970s.

The period of internal factionalism inside the SNP came to an end at the 1982 SNP Conference where internal factions were banned.

The 1980s and the Emergence of Jim Sillars

The 79 Group, despite their proscription were bolstered by the collapse of the Scottish Labour Party (SLP) in the aftermath of the '79 election. This resulted in the SLP's leading figure, Jim Sillars deciding to join the SNP, as did a great number of other ex-SLP members. Sillars had been a Labour Party MP in the 1970s but, dissatisfied with the Labour Government's policy on Scottish devolution and their socio-economic programme, had in 1976 formed the SLP. This influx of ex-SLP members served to strengthen the left of the party, to which these new members naturally gravitated.

In 1979, Billy Wolfe stood down as SNP leader, and in the resultant leadership election Gordon Wilson was elected leader with 530 votes to 79 Group member Stephen Maxwell's 117 votes, and Willie MacRae's 52 votes.

The 1980s offered little hope for the SNP with poor performances in both the 1983 and 1987 General Elections. Indeed even the party leader, Gordon Wilson lost his seat in '87. The party took stock of these results and started to analyse its policy platform. Sillars began to grow in influence in the party and the SNP was firmly placing itself on the left of centre.

Many old-style SNP members believed that the party should be above the old arguments of left and right and should focus solely on the independence argument. Sillars however argued that the Scottish people had to be given reasons as to why independence would benefit their lives and that this should involve a fully developed socio-economic programme. He argued against the idea that somehow the country could be guided in a 'tartan trance' to independence, as if the Scottish people could ignore the realities of the economic system they found themselves in. Sillars was also key in moving the party to adopting a position of *Independence in Europe* to alleviate the 'separatist' tag that the SNP's unionist opponents were ever eager to attach to them. Previously the SNP had been at best highly suspicious about Scotland's continued membership of the EEC, but the new policy which Sillars helped secure firmly committed the SNP to supporting an independent Scotland's membership.

There was a minor setback in 1987 when a few members on the left of the party broke away to establish a Scottish Socialist Party (not the same one that is in existence now), but in the long-run this small party did not establish itself and it folded without threatening to make a major electoral breakthrough.

As the 1980s wore on, the party managed to re-group and in 1988 the SNP managed to win the Govan seat in a by-election for the second time, with Sillars as their candidate. This was a huge upset, as the SNP overturned a Labour majority of around 19,000 and had not been expected to win. However, a hard fought campaign using the party's sizable activist base won through. Sillars oratorial capabilities and street campaigning methods also played a decisive role in the party's victory.

Sillars' victory provoked great alarm amongst the Labour Party hierarchy in Scotland, much as Ewing's had in the 1960s. Fearing that their strong Scottish electoral base was under threat, they helped establish the Scottish Constitutional Convention to set out a blueprint for devolution. Initially the SNP looked as though they would get involved and party leader Gordon Wilson and Sillars attended an initial meeting of the convention. However, the convention's unwillingness to contemplate independence as a constitutional option persuaded Sillars in particular against getting involved and the SNP did not take part.

The 1990s, The First Salmond Era

In 1990 Wilson stood down as leader and was replaced by Alex Salmond, who defeated Margaret Ewing for the post by 486 votes to 186. Salmond's victory surprised many as Ewing had the backing of most of the party leadership, including Sillars and the party secretary at the time, John Swinney, although he would go on to become a key ally of Salmonds. Ewing's prominent supporters made her many people's favourite to win the contest, but in the end Salmond was the convincing victor. He proved a capable leader with his witty and intelligent style of debate giving him a national prominence and boosting the SNP's profile.

In that same year the SNP presence at Westminster was boosted when Labour MP for Dunfermline West, Dick Douglas defected to the SNP, citing his dissatisfaction with the way Labour had handled the Poll Tax issue as one reason. This boosted the SNP numbers at Westminster to five.

The 1992 General Election had promised much for the SNP. It proved to be mixed in fortunes. The SNP held three seats they had won in 1987, but lost Govan. They also lost Dunfermline West, but this was not helped by the sitting MP Dick Douglas deciding to stand against Labour MP Donald Dewar in his Glasgow seat instead of defending the seat he had represented for years.

The SNP had failed to make headway in terms of winning seats. However, their campaign proved a success in terms of votes won, with the SNP vote going up by 50% from their 1987 performance. It proved too much to bear for Sillars though, and he quit active politics, famously describing the Scots as '90 minute patriots'. It also signaled the breakdown of the political relationship between Sillars and Salmond.

The intervening years between the '92 and '97 general elections were marked by some SNP electoral success. In the 1994 elections for the European Parliament the party managed to secure over 30% of the popular vote and return two MEPs (Winnie Ewing and Allan MacCartney). The SNP also came very close to winning the Monklands East by-election of that year, caused by the death of the leader of the Labour Party, John Smith. In 1995 they went one better, when the Perth and Kinross by-election was won by Roseanna Cunningham who later became the party's deputy leader.

The Modern SNP

The 1997 General Election saw the SNP double their number of MPs from three to six and, with the return of the Labour Party to power at that General Election, saw the establishment of a devolved Scottish Parliament. This allowed for the SNP to firmly establish itself as a political force in Scotland with the returning of 35 MSPs in the first Scottish Parliament Election. Later that year the party returned two members of the European Parliament, narrowly missing out on sending a third.

The first term of the Scottish Parliament did not offer the SNP much comfort. Two MSPs quit the party, the aforementioned Margo MacDonald and Dorothy-Grace Elder, citing the actions of some of their colleagues as reasons for their resignations. The SNP also performed poorly at the 2001 General Election, with a reduced share of the vote from 1997, and one less MP.

Despite optimism that the party would at least retain the same number of MSPs they gained in 1999, a downturn in electoral fortune at the 2003 Scottish Parliament Elections has weakened them somewhat. They returned 27 elected members in the Scottish Parliament, making them the second largest party in Holyrood.

The results of the election seem to indicate that the emergence of the Scottish Socialist Party (SSP) and Scottish Green Party (both of whom also support independence) has undermined their vote slightly. It remains to be seen how the SNP will deal with the fact that they are no longer exclusively the party of Scottish independence.

Recent debate within the SNP has been marked by disagreements between the gradualist wing of the party, which believes in taking powers back bit by bit from the UK Parliament and returning them to the Scottish Parliament, as opposed to the viewpoint of the fundamentalist wing. The fundamentalists argue that a greater emphasis should be placed on the party's support for independence to enthuse their activists, as well as their core support. Former leader, Gordon Wilson has publicly stated that he believes it may be that these two wings find their views so irreconcilable that the party may split as a result.

Other political figures often characterise the SNP as trying to be all things to all people. They charge the SNP with trying to appear solidly left-wing in urban Central Scotland where they are trying to unseat the Labour Party, and with appearing more moderate in rural Scotland where their electoral challenge is more often than not against the Conservatives or the Liberal Democrats.

In 2000 John Swinney MSP was elected leader, defeating Alex Neil MSP by 547 votes to 268 in a hotly contested leadership election to replace Alex Salmond as National Convenor.

Swinney's leadership came under challenge, with much press speculation surrounding the future leadership of the SNP by Swinney, with many contrasting his more subdued style of debating technique with that of his charismatic predecessor, Alex Salmond.

This speculation culminated in the challenge for the leadership of the SNP by grassroots activist, Dr. Bill Wilson in the summer of 2003. Wilson was broadly critical of what he argued were the centralising tendencies of the Swinney leadership, as well as a drift to the centre ground of politics away from the SNP's traditional position on the left of Scottish politics. At the party conference of that year the election took place with Swinney receiving 577 of the delegates votes that were cast and Wilson taking 111.

2004 did not get off to a good start for Swinney's leadership. On January 1 a former parliamentary candidate and a party activist in the Shetland Islands Brian Nugent announced that he was forming his own pro-independence party, the "Scottish Party" (which eventually relaunched itself as the Free Scotland Party) in response to what he perceived to be an overly pro-European Union stance by the SNP.

Not long after the party's National Executive Committee decided to firstly suspend, and then expel Campbell Martin, an SNP MSP. Martin had backed Bill Wilson's leadership challenge, and had continued to be overtly critical of Swinney's leadership, resulting in the NEC taking this disciplinary action against him.

Despite a slump in the vote and a decrease in the number of available seats from 7 to 6, the SNP was able to retain its two Members of the European Parliament at the 2004 European elections.

Nonetheless, John Swinney announced his resignation on June 22, 2004. He said that he would remain as caretaker leader until a successor was elected.

2004 Leadership Contest, Salmond Returns

Shortly afterwards, two MSPs (Roseanna Cunningham and Nicola Sturgeon) and one former MSP (Mike Russell) announced that they would be candidates in the election for the party leadership. Alex Neil MSP announced that he would not be a candidate, citing what he believed to be the hostility of senior party figures such as Fergus Ewing and Alex Salmond to the prospect of his becoming leader. In a surprise announcement on July 15, 2004, Alex Salmond announced that he would also be a candidate in the leadership race, despite having previously said "if asked, I'll decline, if nominated, I'll defer, and if elected, I'll resign". Nicola Sturgeon then withdrew from the contest and declared her support for Salmond and decided to stand for Deputy Leader.

This resulted in Kenny MacAskill pulling out of the race for deputy and declaring his support for Salmond and Sturgeon, leaving Sturgeon standing against Fergus Ewing and Christine Grahame. Shortly after Salmond and Sturgeon announced they were running on a joint ticket.

The campaign for leader was characterised by being a low-key affair. Salmond remained firm favourite to win back the leadership of the SNP. There remained greater doubt as to who would be the deputy leader with it being widely expected to be a much more close run affair than that for the post of leader.

There were some surprises during the course of the campaign. Alex Neil and Adam Ingram both came out in support of Alex Salmond, although they supported Grahame for depute rather than Sturgeon. This was unexpected as both men had previously been critics of Salmond in the past. It was particularly surprising in light of Salmond's earlier comments, before he had entered the race that he would have difficulties working with Neil should he be elected leader, although he later went on the record to say that he should not have publicly said this.

There was some degree of criticism of Salmond's position by other candidates, who felt that his decision to lead the SNP from being a member of the British Parliament at Westminster rather than from the Scottish Parliament was contrary to the party's aim of independence. Nonetheless on September 3, 2004 Salmond and Sturgeon were elected leader and deputy respectively. The result of the Leadership contest, in what was the first "One Member One Vote" election run by the SNP (as opposed to the delegate based elections of the past) was Salmond 4,952 (75.8%); Cunningham 953 (14.6%); and Russell 631 (9.7%). The result of the contest for Deputy Leader was Sturgeon 3,521 (53.9%); Ewing 1,605 (24.6%); and Grahame 1,410 (21.6%).

2005 General Election

The SNP had mixed fortunes in the general election held on May 5, 2005. They managed to gain two seats (Angus MacNeil winning in Na h-Eileanan An Iar and Stewart Hosie in Dundee East) from the notional four they held to bring their total to six Members of Parliament. However there was also disappointment in that the sitting MP Annabelle Ewing did not manage to win the new Ochil and South Perthshire constituency, finishing some 600 votes behind the Labour candidate.

There was also disappointment in that the SNP's share of the Scottish vote fell to 17.7% and that they finished third behind the Liberal-Democrats, this was the first time this had ever happened. The SNP's share of the vote across the Scottish Central Belt was particularly low, with some candidates only just managing to achieve a high enough share of the vote in their constituency to retain their £500 deposit.

However, Alex Salmond was in buoyant mood in the aftermath of the campaign, describing the SNP's Westminster parliamentary group as *"Scotland's Super Six"* and also promising that the SNP would be far more competitive in the 2007 election for the Scottish Parliament.

Source (edited): "http://en.wikipedia.org/wiki/History_of_the_Scottish_National_Party"

It's Scotland's oil

North Sea Oil Platforms

It's Scotland's oil was a widely publicised political slogan used by the Scottish National Party (SNP) during the 1970s in making their economic case for Scottish independence. It was argued that the discovery of North Sea oil off the coast of Scotland, and the revenue that it created would not benefit Scotland to any significant degree while Scotland remained part of the United Kingdom.

The SNP campaigned widely in both the February 1974 UK General Election and subsequent October 1974 UK General Election using this slogan. At the February election the SNP gained seven seats in the House of Commons and 22% of the Scottish vote, rising to eleven seats and 30% of the vote in the October election. The idea behind the slogan has proven to be controversial in discussions surrounding the financial viability of an independent Scottish state and still resonates to this day.

Background

The outcome of the February 1974 General Election saw the incumbent Conservative government led by Prime Minister Edward Heath with a plurality of votes in the election, but without a majority of seats in the House of Commons after the withdrawal of support by the Ulster Unionist Party. The Labour Party led by Harold Wilson had four more seats in the House of Commons than the Conservatives, and after the break down of coalition negotiations between Heath and the Liberal leader Jeremy Thorpe, the Labour Party led by Harold Wilson ascended to power governing as a minority administration. In October 1974, Wilson went back to the country to ask for a renewed mandate.

During this time, in Scotland support for the Scottish National Party had been increasing after the seminal victory of the SNP candidate Winnie Ewing at the 1967 Hamilton by-election. The political instability surrounding the general elections of 1974 represented a time of intense political campaigning in the UK, which further brought the SNP to prominence. It was during this time that the slogan "It's Scotland's Oil" came to the fore with the February election seeing 7 SNP candidates returned, rising to 11 in October. Some well known MPs such as Tam Dalyell believe this was in no small part due to the "It's Scotland's oil" slogan employed by the Scottish National Party.

The economic background to the claim was the discovery of oil in the North Sea in the 1960s, and its coming on line in the 1970s. The majority of the largest oil fields in the UK sector of the North Sea were found in the waters to the north and east of the Scottish mainland, with the more northerly fields found to the east of the Orkney and Shetland islands. Aberdeen became the centre of Britain's North Sea oil industry, with many oil terminals such as that of Sullom Voe on Shetland and Flotta on Orkney and at Cruden Bay and St Fergus on the north east coast of Scotland, being built to support the North Sea oil industry. In the early 1970s, there was a great deal of economic turbulence with the 1973 oil price shock caused by the Yom Kippur War, resulting in rising inflation coupled with high unemployment, recession (also known as stagflation) in Scotland and the rest of the United Kingdom. Thus the economic argument that formed the basis of the slogan was that while Scotland was part of the United Kingdom it had no control over royalties and revenue from the majority of the oil which lay in the Scottish sector of the North Sea, and it thus could not be used to benefit of Scotland economically.

Reality of the claim

Given that Scotland is not a sovereign state, it has no effective maritime boundaries; and any claims Scotland may assert are subsumed as part of claims made by the United Kingdom. It could be argued that there is no definitive 'Scottish' sector of the North Sea in the same way there is a Norwegian sector or a Danish sector, or indeed a UK sector. However due to the existence of two separate legal systems in Great Britain — that of Scots law pertaining to Scotland and English law pertaining to England and Wales, constitutional law in the United Kingdom has provided for the division of the UK sector of the North Sea into specific Scottish and English components. The Continental Shelf Act 1964 and the Continental Shelf (Jurisdiction) Order 1968 defines the UK North Sea maritime area to the north of latitude 55 degrees north as being under the jurisdiction of Scots law meaning that 90% of the UK's oil resources were under Scottish jurisdiction. In addition, section 126 of the Scotland Act 1998 defines Scottish waters as *the internal waters and territorial sea of the United Kingdom as are adjacent to Scotland*. This has been subsequently amended by the Scottish Adjacent Waters Boundary Order 1999 which redefined the extent of Scottish waters and Scottish fishery limits.

Recent evidence by Kemp and Stephen (1999) has tried to estimate hypothetical Scottish shares of North Sea Oil revenue by dividing the UK sector of the North Sea into separate Scottish and UK sectors using the international principle of equidistance as utilised under the United Nations Convention on the Law of the Sea (UNCLOS) - such a convention is used in defining the maritime assets of newly formed states and resolving international maritime disputes. The study by Kemp & Stephen showed that hypothesised Scottish shares of North Sea oil revenue over the period 1970 to 1999, varied to as high as 98% dependent upon the price of oil and offset against taxable profits and the costs of exploration and development.

Nevertheless a Scottish share of North Sea oil is never formally alluded to as part of Scotland's net fiscal position and is treated by HM Treasury as *extra-regio* resources. The BBC economist Evan Davis however reported prior to the 2007 Scottish Parliament election that the Barnett formula already allows Scotland to sustain higher levels of per capita public spending relative to the rest of the UK, which is approximately equivalent to its disproportionatly high annual contribution of tax revenues to the central UK Treasury from Oil production. However Scotland's per capita spending growth, relative to the rest of the UK, has in recent years, been nominally reduced by the operation of the Barnett Formula, in order to bring public spending levels into line with the UK average, in a phenomenon that had been dubbed the "Barnett Squeeze".

Recent evidence

Evidence unearthed in late 2005 under the Freedom of Information Act has shown significant UK government concerns over the rising tide of Scottish Nationalism during the early part of the 1970s and the consequences that this may have had upon ownership and control over the UK's North Sea resources. A report written by the Scottish Office economist Gavin McCrone for ministers in 1974 indicated that with ownership of North Sea oil, an independent Scotland would have "embarrassingly" large tax surpluses. The report also stated that the economy of an independent Scotland, with control over the majority of UK North Sea oil revenue, would have one of the "hardest" currencies in Europe and that "for the first time since the Act Of Union was passed, it can now be credibly argued that Scotland's economic advantage lies in its repeal." Source (edited): "http://en.wikipedia.org/wiki/It%27s_Scotland%27s_oil"

Labour Party of Scotland

The **Labour Party of Scotland** were a small political party active in Dundee, Scotland. They were formed as a left-wing breakaway from the Scottish National Party (SNP) and contested the Dundee East by-election, 1973, where the number of votes they gathered, 1409 for their candidate George McLean, were greater than the Labour Party majority over the SNP candidate Gordon Wilson.

The party was wound up not long after the by-election without having made any substantial political impact, with many of their members returning to the SNP.

Former SNP leader, William Wolfe has stated that this breakaway was more to do with local personal political ambition than over any ideological dispute.
Source (edited): "http://en.wikipedia.org/wiki/Labour_Party_of_Scotland"

Moray by-election, 2006

A **by-election** in the **Moray** constituency of the Scottish Parliament was held on 27 April 2006 following the death of the Scottish National Party (SNP) Member of the Scottish Parliament (MSP) Margaret Ewing on 21 March 2006, from breast cancer. The seat was successfully defended by the SNP's Richard Lochhead, increasing the majority over the Scottish Conservative Party by 1073 votes.

Margaret Ewing had held the Holyrood seat since its creation in 1999, having previously represented the Moray constituency as a Westminster Member of Parliament (MP) since the United Kingdom general election, 1987. She had already announced that she would not be contesting the seat in the Scottish Parliament general election, 2007.

Notes on candidates

Richard Lochhead defended the seat for the Scottish National Party. An additional-member MSP for the North East Scotland electoral region since 1999, he had already been selected to contest the seat for the SNP at the Scottish Parliament general election, 2007, beating the incumbent's sister-in-law, former MP Annabelle Ewing. He resigned his list seat to stand in the by-election.

Mary Scanlon, a Conservative MSP for the Highlands and Islands region (which includes Moray), resigned from her list seat to fight as the Conservative candidate. Any sitting MSP intending to fight the by-election must first resign their current seat under section 9 of the Scotland Act.

The Labour candidate was Elgin councillor Sandy Keith. He saw his party's vote share fall in the by-election, resulting in increases for all the other parties.

The Liberal Democrat candidate was Linda Gorn, came fourth when she fought the seat in 2003 but improved her performance substantially in the by-election, moving to third place not far behind the Conservative candidate and increasing her share of the vote more than any other candidate.

The Scottish Socialist Party announced that they would not be entering a candidate. They decided that they, in common with the Scottish Green Party, will concentrate on campaigning for regional list votes (Additional member system) at the next Scottish Parliament general election, 2007.

Melville Brown, a former Conservative Party candidate for Edinburgh East, stood for the NHSFirst Party, the first time the party has contested an election. Brown is the party chairman.

Campaign controversies

The Conservative Party became embroiled in a row with local two local independent councillors. Handwritten notes were sent out in their wards allegedly from the councillors, but the councillors subsequently denied having given permission for the letters to be used..

The following week, a local newspaper, the *Northern Scot*, reported the Liberal Democrats to the Electoral Commission for attributing quotes in leaflets to the newspaper itself rather than to the specific Liberal Democrats whom the paper had been quoting.

Both of the above were given widespread coverage in the *Northern Scot* newspaper.

In the final week of the by-election, Robbie Rowantree, the Conservative Party candidate for the neighbouring UK Parliament constituency of Inverness, Nairn, Badenoch and Strathspey in the 2005 general election, announced he was joining the Liberal Democrats.
Source (edited): "http://en.wikipedia.org/wiki/Moray_by-election,_2006"

National Conversation

The **National Conversation** was the name given to the Scottish Government's public consultation exercise regarding possible future changes in the power of the devolved Scottish Parliament and the possibility of Scottish independence, a policy objective of the Scottish National Party, who at the time were the minority government with power over devolved affairs in Scotland, as the Scottish Government. It culminated in a multi-option white paper for a proposed Referendum (Scotland) Bill, 2010.

Process

The National Conversation was launched on 14 August 2007 by Alex Salmond, the First Minister of Scotland. It consisted of a 59 page white paper, titled Choosing Scotland's Future, and a website. The white paper included a draft bill for a referendum to allow for negotiations with the UK Government on Scottish independence. The website encourages comments to be made on the white paper. Comments are encouraged from members of the public, rather than just interest groups.

As a culmination to the National

Conversation, a white paper for the proposed Referendum (Scotland) Bill, 2010 was published on St. Andrew's Day on 30 November 2009. The 176 page paper was titled, "Your Scotland, Your Voice". The paper detailed four possible scenarios for Scotland's future, with the text of the Bill and Referendum to be revealed later. The scenarios were: No Change, Devolution per the Calman Review, Full Devolution, and Full Independence.

Response

On 6 December 2007, the Scottish Parliament voted to create a Commission on Scottish Devolution, chaired by Sir Kenneth Calman, and with the remit:
To review the provisions of the Scotland Act 1998 in the light of experience and to recommend any changes to the present constitutional arrangements that would enable the Scottish Parliament to serve the people of Scotland better, improve the financial accountability of the Scottish Parliament, and continue to secure the position of Scotland within the United Kingdom.
The Commission was supported by the three main pro-Union political parties in Scotland: Labour, Conservatives and Liberal Democrats. Wendy Alexander, at the time leader of the Labour party in the Scottish Parliament, proposed the motion, rejecting the National Conversation and an amendment proposed by the Scottish National Party calling for support for the National Conversation was defeated, Ms Alexander associating it with moves towards Scottish independence and making the following response:
The SNP amendment predictably calls for us to participate in the National Conversation, but how can the SNP possibly claim to be leading a conversation when it has already decided what the only acceptable outcome will be? Worst of all, it has no parliamentary mandate whatsoever for the conversation. How can the SNP possibly justify the use of taxpayers' money on something that is little more than propaganda?
Notably the remit of the Commission on Scottish Devolution precludes the consideration of Scottish independence.

The rejection of the National Conversation by the Scottish Parliament has led to criticisms as to its legitimacy. Concerns have also been raised by

Website controversy

On 24 April 2008, Lord Foulkes, a Labour Member of the Scottish Parliament, claimed that the National Conversation had been met with "complete indifference" by the people of Scotland, quoting website visiting figures. He further claimed that the website had become a meeting place for SNP activists, noting also that although 41 comments had been removed from the site, "there are still anti-English remarks bordering on racism."

Influence

The initiative influenced the Parti Québécois and, in March 2008, shortly before the Parti Québécois National Council, leader Pauline Marois presented the party's plan to propose a *conversation nationale* to Quebecers as part of Marois' renewal of the party's approach on independence and social democracy. In this case, however, the conversation is to be solely on independence, instead of three options. The expression was met with less enthusiasm in Quebec and arose cynicism in the press and objection with some party hardliners. Shorty after, the Parti Québécois replaced the term with *débat sur la souveraineté* ("debate on sovereignty").
Source (edited): "http://en.wikipedia.org/wiki/National_Conversation"

Orkney and Shetland Movement

The **Orkney and Shetland Movement** was an electoral coalition formed for the 1987 general election. The pro-devolution Orkney Movement and Shetland Movement agreed on selecting John Goodlad, the secretary of the Shetland Fishermen's Association, as a joint candidate for the Orkney and Shetland constituency, and the Scottish National Party agreed to stand aside in favour of the coalition.

Their candidate won 3,095 votes, which represented 14.5% of the vote in the small seat, but came fourth, just behind the Labour Party, the best result at the time for a candidate not from one of the four main parties in Scotland.

They took part in the 1989 Scottish Constitutional Convention that developed a framework for the eventual Scottish devolution in 1999.
Source (edited): "http://en.wikipedia.org/wiki/Orkney_and_Shetland_Movement"

Radio Free Scotland

Between 1956-1965 **Radio Free Scotland** (RFS) broadcast through the sound channel of BBC television after *God Save the Queen* finished in the evening, and, later on, on 262 meters medium wave on the radio.

The first broadcast interrupted a BBC newscast when viewers in Perth were told to stay tuned following sign off. This "pirate" radio transmission opened with the provocative statement: "This is Radio Free Scotland proclaiming to the nation that the fight for independence is on in earnest". This roving station was heard for almost a month in Glasgow, Ayrshire and Perth. The Scottish National Party announced official backing for Radio Free Scotland because of the government ban on broadcasts by the Scottish and Welsh nationalists on the BBC.

The BBC later paid for the right to re-broadcast some RFS material and the SNP and Plaid Cymru gained the right, as other parties already had, to time on mainstream broadcasters.

Leading figures in Radio Free Scotland included "Controller General", Gordon Wilson, who later became an MP (1974–1987) and was Chairman (Convener) of the SNP from 1979 to 1990. Douglas Henderson, also later an MP, was "Director of Programmes" between 1963-1965. Scotland's oldest woman when she died, Annie Knight, hosted the station in her living room during 1962.

Radio Free Scotland was re-launched in 2007 to help support Self Determination for Scotland in the Elections in May 2008. With Pax and Kevin Williamson presenting the shows and Friseal as webmaster. The shows took a hiatus for 18 months until recently and will be back "on air" soon. In keeping with the original Radio Free Scotland the opening lines from the original broadcasts are still used. The website is under construction but a holding page can be found at http://www.radiofreescotland.com and if funded via donations from all walks of independent minded Scots.

Source (edited): "http://en.wikipedia.org/wiki/Radio_Free_Scotland"

Referendum (Scotland) Bill, 2010

The **Referendum Bill 2010** was (and to some extent is) a proposed Scottish Government bill to set out the arrangements for a potential referendum of the Scottish electorate on the issue of Scottish independence from the United Kingdom, to be held in November 2010. However, on 7 September 2010 the Scottish National Party led Government announced that they were withdrawing their plan for a referendum before the 2011 elections.

When plans for the Bill were announced in August 2009, it was not believed it would be passed into law, hence preventing any referendum, due to the lack of support for it by the major opposition parties in the Scottish Parliament. However, the Bill is the centrepiece of the governing Scottish National Party's legislative programme for 2009-10, with the next elections to the Scottish Parliament expected in May 2011. A white paper for the Bill, setting out four possible options ranging from no change and full Independence, was published on 30 November 2009.

A draft bill for public consultation was published on 25 February 2010, setting out a two question yes/no referendum, proposing both further devolution, and full independence. Rather than an independence referendum, the main opposition parties in Scotland have been supporting the Commission on Scottish Devolution (the Calman Review) process, whose recommendations have had the support of the British government in Westminster, both before and after the change in administration resulting from the May 2010 United Kingdom general election.

Background

Past referendums

A referendum on Scottish devolution was held in 1997; though that did not broach the issue of independence, sufficient support for a devolved Parliament was gained. A less wide ranging proposal was also put to a referendum in 1979, but resulted in no change.

2007 SNP administration

Scottish First Minister Alex Salmond and Deputy First Minister Nicola Sturgeon at the launch of the National Conversation, 14 August 2007

A commitment to hold a referendum in 2010 was part of the Scottish National Party's election manifesto when it contested the May 2007 Scottish Parliament election. As a result of that election, it became the largest party in the Scottish Parliament for the first time, and formed a minority administration in the Scottish Executive, the devolved legislative assembly first established in 1999 for dealing with unreserved matters within Scotland. Rebranding the Scottish Executive as the Scottish Government, the SNP administration accordingly launched a 'National Conversation' as a consultation exercise in August 2007, part of which included a draft of a referendum bill, as the *Referendum (Scotland) Bill*.

After forming the Scottish Government in 2007, the SNP had a long standing policy of not holding any referendum until 2010, so as to be well into its term. A call by Wendy Alexander in May 2008, the then leader of the Scottish Labour Party, for the SNP to begin debate on the referendum issue early was rejected by the SNP, and she resigned in June 2008 over a donations row, and the call was not made again by Labour.

Opposition stance

In December 2007, the main Scottish opposition parties backed the UK Government's plan for creation of the Commission on Scottish Devolution (the Calman Review), chaired by Sir Kenneth Calman, to look into options for further devolution, but ruling out full independence. The Calman Commission reported in June 2009 shortly before the plans for a Referendum Bill were announced, leading to an alternative process in parallel to the SNP's plans for a referendum, running without their participation.

Ongoing political context

Debating chamber of the Scottish Parliament

At the time the plans for a referendum were announced in early September 2009, only the Scottish Green Party with two MSPs supported the SNP, who number 47 of the total of 129 MSPs. All the other major parties in Parliament, the Scottish Labour Party (46 MSPs), the Scottish Conservative Party (16 MSPs) and Scottish Liberal Democrats (16 MSPs) intended to oppose the Bill. A previous non-binding vote on the issue of a referendum held in March 2009, tabled by the Liberal Democrats as an amendment to a Labour debate on the economy, was defeated with a 25-vote majority (47-72).

Due to the opposition from other main Scottish Parliament groups and the SNP's status as a minority administration, it was not expected that the SNP would be able to get the Referendum Bill passed into law when ultimately presented to the Scottish Parliament for debate, meaning that the referendum would not be able to be held. It has been speculated that if the Bill was defeated, Scottish independence would become a defining issue of the planned Scottish Parliament election in May 2011.

History

Legislative plans announced

The legislative plans for the Referendum Bill were announced in late August/early September 2009 by the SNP government, intended to be the centrepiece of their 2009-2010 proposed parliamentary programme, their third legislative session of their 2007.

2009 party conferences

At the annual Labour national Party Conference in Brighton in September 2009, the Scottish Labour Leader Iain Gray attacked the SNP's proposed referendum, stating that time was not right for a referendum, that Alex Salmond had "no mandate, no majority and no shame", and that the only choice for Scottish voters in the next UK general election was between Labour and the Conservatives.

Scottish Liberal Democrat Leader Tavish Scott reaffirmed their opposition to a referendum at the Liberal Democrat's annual UK party conference in Bournemouth in September 2009. On 8 October 2009 it was announced that senior MSP Ross Finnie would conduct a review of their position, and a consultation session would be held at the Party's autumn conference in Dunfermline. On 1 November, following the conference, Tavish Scott re-affirmed their stance to oppose the proposed Referendum Bill, but confirmed that the party would continue to review options for a different type of referendum for its 2011 Scottish Parliament election manifesto.

Opening the SNP annual party conference in Inverness on 15 October 2009, Alex Salmond declared "Do parties in Scotland really believe that the people of Scotland will give them their votes if they refuse to give the people of Scotland a vote on the constitutional future of the country?", while outlining his hopes to form a Scottish voting block of at least 20 SNP MPs in the next UK general election, to gain influence for Scotland in the event of a hung parliament. When a hung parliament occurred as a result of the United Kingdom General Election 2010, the SNP failed to form part of the governing coalition.

Calman Review white paper published

On 25 November 2009, based on the findings of the Calman Commission, the UK Labour Government published a white paper on a proposed Scotland Bill. This detailed new powers would be devolved to the Scottish Government, notably on how it can raise tax and carry out capital borrowing, and the running of Scottish Parliament elections. These proposals were detailed in a white paper setting out a new Scotland Bill, to become law before the 2015 Holyrood elections.

The proposal was criticised by the then UK parliament opposition parties for not proposing to implement any changes before the next United Kingdom general election. The SNP Scottish Constitution Minister Michael Russell criticised the white paper, calling it "flimsy" and stating the proposed Referendum Bill, whose own white paper was to be published five days later, would be "more substantial". According to *The Independent*, the Calman Review white paper proposals fall short of what would normally be seen as requiring a referendum.

Referendum Bill white paper published

As a culmination to the National Conversation, a white paper for the proposed Referendum Bill was published on St. Andrew's Day on 30 November 2009. The 176 page paper was titled, "Your Scotland, Your Voice". The paper detailed four possible scenarios, with the text of the Bill and Referendum to be revealed later. The scenarios were: No Change, Devolution per the Calman Review, Full Devolution, and Full Independence. The Full Devolution option, while short of Independence, would make the Scottish Parliament responsible for the 'vast majority' of tax and spending in Scotland, with a remittance paid to the UK to "cover common UK public goods and services such as defence and foreign affairs." The paper acknowledged that while the SNP government did not support anything other than full independence, the Referendum Bill would have provisions for a multi-option referendum, and called on opposition parties to propose a suitable form for these options, which had according to the paper been shown by the National Conversation to have support in Scotland.

Draft Bill published for consultation

The Scottish Government published a draft version of the bill on Burns night, 25 February 2010, for public consultation. The 84 page document was titled *Scotland's Future: Draft Referendum (Scotland) Bill Consultation Paper* and contained a consultation document and a draft version of the bill. The consultation paper set out the proposed ballot papers, the mechanics of the proposed referendum, and how the proposed referendum was to be regulated. Public responses were invited from February 25 to April 30.

2010 United Kingdom general election

The UK general election was due to take place on or before 3 June 2010, before the Scottish Parliament elections due in May 2011. It was eventually called on 6 May 2010, and while the SNP hoped for influence in a hung parliament, the election instead led to a change in Westminster from a Labour majority government under Gordon Brown to a Conservative / Liberal Democrat coalition government, the first British coalition since the Second World War, with David Cameron as Prime Minister. The SNP failed however to increase their number of Westminster seats, falling well short of their declared target of 20, albeit holding their 6 constituencies won in 2005 but losing heavily to Labour in the Glasgow East seat won in a 2008 by-election.

Post election

After the change in government following the 2010 general election, the new Conservative / Liberal Democrat coalition government committed itself in its May 2010 Coalition Agreement to implementing the proposals of the Calman Commission. It was believed that this new Scotland Bill could be introduced as early as the Autumn. On 31 May 2010 the Scottish Liberal Democrats invited the SNP to join the steering group brought together to oversee its implementation, which the SNP had thus far refused to participate in, with the offer of a 'Calman Plus' type package, similar to the 'devolution max' proposal included in the draft referendum bill.

On 6 June 2010 the Scottish Government published 189 of the 222 responses received during the draft bill consultation period.

Draft Bill details

Ballot procedure

The draft bill outlines a referendum posing two yes/no questions to the electorate. Voting would be held in a single day, and can be in person at a polling booth, by proxy, or by post. Votes would be counted by hand, and a national declaration of the result would then be made. A 'yes' result for either question would be determined by simple majority, i.e. more than 50%.

The referendum questions are to be presented as 'Proposal 1' and 'Proposal 2', to be presented on separate, differently coloured, ballot papers. The first proposal is whether there should be an extension of the powers and responsibilities of the Scottish Parliament, short of independence; while the second is whether the Scottish Parliament should "also have its powers extended to enable independence to be achieved". Voters are to be allowed to vote on both proposals, by placing an X in a box against either, "Yes, I agree", or "No, I do not agree", on each ballot paper.

Two possible versions for the wording of Proposal 1 were presented for consultation, one proposing an extension of power based on the financial recommendations of the Calman Commission, the other proposing full devolution with only some matters left to the UK parliament (sometimes called "devolution max").

Ballot paper

Proposal 1: Additional Powers

Version 1 of Proposal 1, outlining full devolution or 'devolution max', proposes that the Scottish Parliament should be responsible for "all laws, taxes and duties in Scotland.", with the exception of "defence and foreign affairs; financial regulation, monetary policy and the currency.", which would be retained by the UK government.

Titled "Increased powers and responsibilities for Scotland", it states:

- **The Scottish Parliament should have its powers and responsibilities extended as described above.**

Version 2 of Proposal 1, outlining Calman type fiscal reform, proposes that the Scottish Parliament should gain the additional powers and responsibilities of setting a Scottish rate of income tax that could vary by up to 10p in the pound compared to the rest of the UK, setting the rate of stamp duty land tax and "other minor taxes", and introducing new taxes in Scotland with the agreement of the UK Parliament, and finally, "limited power to borrow money."

Titled "Increased financial powers and responsibilities for Scotland", it states:

- **The Scottish Parliament should have its financial powers and responsibilities extended as recommended by the Commission on Scottish Devolution.**

Proposal 2: Full Independence

Proposal 2, outlining the option for full independence, proposes that the Scottish Parliament would gain the powers to be able to convert Scotland into a country which would "have the rights and responsibilities of a normal, sovereign state". This state would be a full Member State of the European Union, with the consequent social and economic relationship with the remainder of the UK which is already a member. Queen Elizabeth would remain as Scotland's head of state, while the United Kingdom would "become a monarchical and social Union – united kingdoms rather than a United Kingdom – maintaining a relationship forged in 1603 by the Union of the Crowns". The currency of Scotland would remain as the pound sterling (£) unless or until the Scottish electorate chose to adopt the Euro (€), which would be left to a separate referendum.

Titled "Additional power to enable Scotland to become an independent country", it states:

- **The Scottish Government proposes that, in addition to the extension of the powers and responsibilities of the Scottish Parliament set out in Proposal 1, the Parliament's powers should also be extended to enable independence to be achieved.**

Eligibility

The following people would be entitled to vote in the referendum:
- British citizens resident in Scotland;
- Commonwealth citizens resident in Scotland;
- Republic of Ireland citizens resident in Scotland;
- citizens of other EU countries resident in Scotland;
- members of the House of Lords resident in Scotland;
- Service/Crown personnel serving in the UK or overseas in the armed forces or with Her Majesty's Government who are registered to vote in Scotland.

People aged 16 or 17 will be allowed to vote if registered on the date of the poll, in-line with the Scottish Government's desire to reduce the voting age in Scotland to 16.

Referendum Commission

The Scottish Government proposes to set up the Scottish Referendum Commission to oversee the referendum, whose members would be "nominated by, and accountable to, the Scottish Parliament." The commission was to be "with limited exceptions, be completely independent of the Scottish Parliament and Government in the conduct of its affairs", and be modelled on the UK's Electoral Commission. The rules on how to conduct the poll and campaigns for the referendum would be based on existing UK legislation, being broadly formed from the Political Parties, Elections and Referendums Act 2000. A Chief Counting Officer for the poll would be appointed by Scottish ministers, and be selected from an existing or former Scottish election Returning Officer.

Campaign funding

For each specific proposal outcome that can be campaigned for, there would be allowed to exist one 'designated organisation', permitted to spend up to £750,000 on their campaign, including expenses, but they would also be entitled to one free mailshot to every household or voter in the poll. Political parties represented in the Scottish Parliament would be limited to a campaign budget of £100,000 including expenses, in addition to any activity through affiliation with one of the designated organisations.

Referendum date

The SNP plan as of September 2009 was for the referendum to be held on or about 30 November 2010, a significant date to Scottish national identity, being St. Andrew's Day.

Cost

According to the Scottish Government's consultation paper published on 25 February 2010, the cost of holding the referendum is "likely to be around £9.5 million", mostly spent on running the poll and the count. Costs would also include the posting of one neutral information leaflet about the referendum to every Scottish household, and one free mailshot to every household or voter in the poll for the 'designated organisations' (See #Campaign funding). There is to be no public funding for campaigns, which would also be subject to spending limits.

Potential consequences

Under the current system of devolution for Scotland, the Scottish Government does not have within its remit the power to declare independence from the United Kingdom, with the constitution being a reserved matter for the supreme legislative body in the UK, the Parliament of the United Kingdom, based in Westminster, London. According to the Scottish Government, the proposed referendum is therefore an "advisory referendum on extending the powers of the Scottish Parliament", whose result "will have no legal effect on [the United Kingdom]."

According to the Scottish Government's consultation paper published on 25 February 2010, if there was a 'yes, yes' outcome of the poll, then following the "necessary negotiations" between the Scottish and UK governments, "it would then be for the Scottish and UK Parliaments to act on the expressed will of the Scottish people". If there was a yes vote for Proposal 1 (further devolution) but not Proposal 2 (powers for independence), then depending on the measures voted for, they would be implemented by Order-in-Council, Sewel Motion, or a combination of the two.

With regard to legislative competence, the Scottish Government believes that Scottish Parliamentary consideration of a referendum bill, in its proposed draft form, is legitimate, under the built in flexibility of the Scotland Act 1998.
Source (edited): "http://en.wikipedia.org/wiki/Referendum_(Scotland)_Bill,_2010"

SNP Trade Union Group

The **SNP Trade Union Group (TUG)** is an affiliated organisation of the Scottish National Party (SNP). They were formed in the 1960s as the **Association of Scottish Nationalist Trade Unionists** to persuade Scottish trade unionists of the virtues of Scottish independence and to ensure the SNP has an organised presence in the trade union movement.

The TUG is allowed to send delegates to the SNP Annual National Conference and National Council meetings, and has one representative on the National Executive Committee (NEC).
Source (edited): "http://en.wikipedia.org/wiki/SNP_Trade_Union_Group"

SNP fundamentalist

The **fundamentalist** ideology within the Scottish National Party (SNP) is the belief that the SNP should emphasise its policy of Scottish independence more widely in order to achieve it. The argument goes that if the SNP is unprepared to argue for its central policy then it is unlikely ever to persuade the public of its worthiness.

Many fundamentalists (including Jim Sillars) were extremely wary of supporting the establishment of the devolved Scottish Parliament as they believed it had been designed to limit the aspirations of those who desire independence. Sillars used his column in *The Sun* to make clear such concerns and accordingly advised people to abstain from voting in the 1997 referendum which endorsed the principle of devolution.

Source (edited): "http://en.wikipedia.org/wiki/SNP_fundamentalist"

SNP gradualist

The **gradualist** viewpoint within the Scottish National Party (SNP) is the idea that Scottish independence can be won by the accumulation by the Scottish Parliament of powers that the UK Parliament currently has over a protracted period of time. It is also a philosophy that emphasises the election of an SNP government should bring about trust in the Scottish people in the ability of Scotland to govern herself, thus bringing increased support for independence. Gradualism comes from the Parti Québécois strategy for the independence of Quebec, étapisme.

Gradualism stands in opposition to the so called 'fundamentalist' point of view that would stress the SNP's support of independence more, and appear to have coined the term 'fundamentalist' too. Critics of gradualism maintain that it allows the UK parliament to dictate Scotland's status, rather than allowing people in Scotland itself to self-determine.

Most political commentators today acknowledge that the current SNP leadership is by and large of the gradualist mould.

Source (edited): "http://en.wikipedia.org/wiki/SNP_gradualist"

Scots National League

The **Scots National League** (SNL) were a body seeking Scottish independence in the early 1920s. They were formed in 1921 largely at the efforts of Ruairidh Erskine of Mar and William Gillies.

The SNL suffered due to it being primarily based in London and during its first few years often spent more time discussing the Irish situation than the Scottish. The group was accused of being anti-English.

The SNL was largely influenced by Sinn Féin and advocated the removal of elected Scottish nationalist MPs from the Westminster Parliament to set up an independent Scottish Parliament.

The SNL established the Scots Independent newspaper in 1926 to further their aims. In 1928 they helped form the National Party of Scotland (NPS) and merged themselves into that party.

By the time of the formation of the NPS the SNL had outgrown its London roots and become stronger in Scotland, largely due to the influence of Tom Gibson. Gibson had realised that nationalist politics needed to be connected to everyday issues in order to become popular. This strain of thought was prominent within the NPS and many SNL members drifted from it due to their belief that the NPS was too moderate. This included Ruairidh Erskine himself who drifted totally from politics.

Source (edited): "http://en.wikipedia.org/wiki/Scots_National_League"

Scots Wha Hae

Scots Wha Hae ("Scots, Who Have"; Scottish Gaelic: *Brosnachadh Bhruis*) is a patriotic song of Scotland which served for a long time as an unofficial national anthem of the country, but has lately been largely supplanted by *Scotland the Brave* and *Flower of Scotland*.

The lyrics were written by Robert Burns in 1793, in the form of a speech given by Robert the Bruce before the Battle of Bannockburn in 1314, where Scotland maintained its sovereignty from the Kingdom of England. Although the lyrics are by Burns, he wrote them to the traditional Scottish tune *Hey Tuttie Tatie* which, according to tradition, was played by Bruce's army at the Battle of Bannockburn, and by the Franco-Scots army at the Siege of Orleans.

The tune tends to be played as a slow air, but certain arrangements put it at a faster tempo, as in the *Scottish Fantasy* by Max Bruch and the concert overture *Rob Roy* by Hector Berlioz.

The song was sent by Burns to his publisher George Thomson, at the end of August 1793, with the title *Robert Bruce's March To Bannockburn*, and a postscript saying that he had been inspired by Bruce's 'glorious struggle for Freedom, associated with the glowing ideas of some other struggles of the same nature, not quite so ancient.' This is seen as a covert reference to the Radical movement, and particularly to the trial of the Glasgow lawyer Thomas Muir of Huntershill, whose trial began on 30 August 1793 as part of a British government crackdown, after the French Revolutionary Wars led to France declaring war on the Kingdom of Great Britain on 1 February 1793.

Muir was accused of sedition for allegedly inciting the Scottish people to oppose the government during the December 1792 convention of the Scottish 'Friends of the People' society, and was eventually sentenced to fourteen years transportation to the convict settlement at Botany Bay, Australia.

Burns was aware that if he declared his Republican and Radical sympathies openly he could suffer the same fate. It is notable that when Burns agreed to let the *Morning Chronicle*, of 8 May 1794, publish the song, it was on the basis of 'let them insert it as a thing they have met with by accident, and unknown to me.'

The song was included in the 1799 edition of *A Select Collection of Original Scottish Airs for the Voice*, edited by George Thomson, but Thomson preferred the tune "Lewie Gordon" and had Burns add to the fourth line of each stanza, to suit. In the 1802 edition, the original words and tune were restored.

"Scots Wha Hae" is the party song of the Scottish National Party. It is sung at the close of their annual national conference each year.

Source (edited): "http://en.wikipedia.org/wiki/Scots_Wha_Hae"

Scottish Labour Party (1976)

The **Scottish Labour Party** (SLP) was formed on January 18, 1976, as a breakaway from the UK Labour Party, by members disaffected with the then Labour Government's failure to secure a devolved Scottish Assembly, as well as with its social and economic agenda. The formation of the SLP was led by Jim Sillars, then MP for South Ayrshire, John Robertson, then MP for Paisley and Alex Neil, the UK Labour Party's senior Scottish researcher. By 1979 the Scottish Labour Party had lost its seats in the House of Commons, and in 1981 it was formally disbanded.

Almost immediately the SLP became the focus for entryism from the International Marxist Group (IMG), and at the party's first congress in October 1976 the IMG was expelled, along with a number of branches whose members were not associated with the IMG. According to Henry Drucker's account, the IMG's role was rather limited; Sillars used this as an excuse for purging anyone he did not see entirely eye-to-eye with or represented a significant threat to his leadership.

The expellees formed a rival Scottish Labour Party (Democratic Wing), and this in turn later renamed itself the Scottish Socialist League (SSL). Gradually, those members of the SSL who had not been associated with the IMG drifted out, and the SSL was reabsorbed into the Trotskyist Fourth International.

The SLP had little electoral success, winning only three council seats at the Scottish district council elections, 1977. It polled only 583 votes in the Garscadden by-election in 1978. At the 1979 UK general election, the SLP fought three seats, including Sillars' attempt at being re-elected (Robertson chose to step down). Sillars came close to retaining his seat in South Ayrshire, but this was clearly a personal vote built up over the years he had already served as an MP, as the other two candidates polled poorly indeed.

This failure prompted the SLP to disband; and members either fell out of active politics, re-joined the Labour Party, or chose to join the Scottish National Party (SNP), which both Sillars and Neil did, with both rising to high office in the SNP.

The SLP adventure is generally looked upon as an ambitious failure, but Sillars has himself put this down to a lack of planning before the decision to launch the party. Unlike the SLP, the Social Democratic Party (SDP) meticulously planned their breakaway from the Labour Party, and were much more successful. Sillars has claimed that the SLP did at least provide a forerunner to the SNP's later dialogue with the left.

The SLP had a number of members who would later go on to achieve a name for themselves as a mainstream Labour politician, including John McAllion who became MP and then MSP for Dundee East, Maria Fyfe one time MP for Glasgow Maryhill, Colin Boyd, the former Lord Advocate, and Charlie Gordon, the current MSP for Glasgow Cathcart. These individuals chose to join (or in some cases re-join) the Labour Party rather than follow Sillars into the SNP.

Source (edited): "http://en.wikipedia.org/wiki/Scottish_Labour_Party_(1976)"

Scottish National Party

The **Scottish National Party** (SNP; Scottish Gaelic: *Pàrtaidh Nàiseanta na h-Alba*; Scots: *Scottis Naitional Pairtie*) is a centre-left, social-democratic political party in Scotland which campaigns for the independence of Scotland from the United Kingdom. The party's stated aim is "to create a just, caring and enterprising society by releasing Scotland's full potential as a sovereign state in the mainstream of modern Europe." Having won 47 of the 129 seats in the 2007 Scottish Parliamentary election, the SNP is currently the largest political party in Scotland and governs as a minority administration, with party leader Alex Salmond as First Minister.

The SNP was founded in 1934, and has had continuous parliamentary representation since Winnie Ewing's groundbreaking victory at the 1967 Hamilton by-election. The SNP currently holds 6 of 59 Scottish seats in the UK Parliament and 2 of 6 Scottish seats in the European Parliament. The SNP is also currently the largest group in Scottish local government and, in coalition, forms 12 out of 32 local administrations.

History

The SNP was formed in 1934 from the merger of the National Party of Scotland and the Scottish Party. Professor Douglas Young, who was the leader of the Scottish National Party from 1942 to 1945 fought for the Scottish people to refuse conscription and his activities were popularly vilified as undermining the British war effort against the Nazis. Young was imprisoned for refusing to be conscripted. The SNP first won a parliamentary seat at the Motherwell by-election in 1945, but Dr Robert McIntyre MP lost the seat at the general election three months later. They next won a seat in 1967, when Winnie Ewing was the surprise winner of a by-election in the previously safe Labour seat of Hamilton. This brought the SNP to national prominence, leading to the establishment of the Kilbrandon Commission. The high point in a British General Elections thus far was when the SNP polled almost a third of all votes in Scotland at the October 1974 general election and returned 11 MPs to Westminster, to date the most MPs it has had.

Party leaders

- Alexander MacEwan (1934–1936)
- Andrew Dewar Gibb (1936–1940)
- William Power (1940–1942)
- Douglas Young (1942–1945)
- Bruce Watson (1945–1947)
- Robert McIntyre (1947–1956)
- James Halliday (1956–1960)
- Arthur Donaldson (1960–1969)
- William Wolfe (1969–1979)
- Gordon Wilson (1979–1990)
- Alex Salmond (1990–2000)
- John Swinney (2000–2004)
- Alex Salmond (2004–present)

Scottish parliamentary leaders

- Alex Salmond (1999–2000)
- John Swinney (2000–2004)
- Nicola Sturgeon (2004–2007)
- Alex Salmond (2007–present)

Westminster parliamentary leader

- Angus Robertson (2007–present)

Party organisation

The SNP consists of local branches of party members. Those branches then form an association in the constituency they represent (unless there is only one branch in the constituency, in which case it forms a constituency branch rather than a constituency association). There are also eight regional associations, to which the branches and constituency associations can send delegates.

The SNP's policy structure is developed at its annual national conference and its regular national council meetings. There are also regular meetings of its national assembly, at which detailed discussion (but not finalising) of party policy takes place.

The party has an active youth wing as well as a student wing. There is also an SNP Trade Union Group. There is an independently-owned monthly newspaper, *The Scots Independent*, which is highly supportive of the party.

The SNP's leadership is vested in its National Executive Committee (NEC) which is made up of the party's elected office bearers and six elected members (voted for at conference). The SNP parliamentarians (Scottish, Westminster and European) and councillors have representation on the NEC, as do the Trade Union Group, the youth wing and the student wing.

According to accounts filed with the Electoral Commission for the year ending 2008, the party had a membership of 15,097 in 2008, up from 9,450 in 2003. In 2004 the party had income of approximately £1,300,000 (including bequests of just under £300,000) and expenditure of about £1,000,000.

Policy platform

The SNP's policy base is mostly in the mainstream European social-democratic mould. For example, among its policies are a commitment to unilateral nuclear disarmament, progressive personal taxation and the eradication of poverty, free state education including support grants for higher education students and a pay increase for nurses. It is also committed to an independent Scotland being a full member state of the European Union, to the country joining the single European currency at the appropriate exchange rate and is against membership of NATO (however this remains controversial).

Contrary to the expectations of many outside the party, the SNP is not expressly republican, and its general view is that this is an issue secondary to that of Scottish independence. Many SNP members are republicans, however, and both the party student and youth wings are expressly so.

In August 2009 as part of its third legislative term in the Scottish Parliament, the Government proposes to debate the Scottish referendum bill 2010, which would set out a planned referendum for 30th November 2010 on the issue of Scottish independence. It was not however expected to pass, due to opposition from all the major opposition parties in the Parliament.

Party ideology

Although it has a representative majority of moderate left-of-centre politicians, this has not always been the case. Almost from the party's foundation there have been internal ideological tensions. This was largely a product of the way in which the left-of-centre National Party of Scotland amalgamated with the right-of-centre Scottish Party. Nowadays, ideological tensions within the SNP have been partially resolved.

However, by the 1960s, the party was starting to become defined ideologically. It had by then established a National Assembly which allowed for discussion of policy and was producing papers on a host of policy issues that could be described as social democratic. Also, the emergence of William Wolfe (universally known as Billy) as a leading figure played a huge role in the SNP defining itself as a left-of-centre social-democratic party. He recognised the need to do this to challenge the dominant political position of the Scottish Labour Party.

He achieved this in a number of ways: establishing the SNP Trade Union Group; promoting left-of-centre policies; and identifying the SNP with labour campaigns (such as the Upper-Clyde Shipbuilders Work-in and the attempt of the workers at the Scottish *Daily Express* to run as a cooperative). It was during Wolfe's period as SNP leader in the 1970s that the SNP became clearly identified as a social-democratic political party.

There were some ideological tensions in the 1970s SNP. The party leadership under Wolfe was determined to stay on the left of the Scottish political spectrum and be in a position to challenge Labour. However, the party's MPs, mostly representing seats won from the Conservatives, were less keen to have the SNP viewed as a left-of-centre alternative to Labour, for fear of losing their seats back to the Conservatives.

There were further ideological and internal struggles after 1979 with the 79 Group attempting to move the SNP further to the left, away from being what could be described a 'social-democratic' party, to an expressly 'socialist' party. 79 Group members including current leader, Alex Salmond, were expelled from the party. This produced a response in the shape of the Campaign for Nationalism in Scotland from those who wanted the SNP to remain a 'broad church', apart from arguments of left vs. right.

The 1980s saw the SNP further define itself as a party of the left, for example running campaigns against the poll tax. It developed this platform to the stage it is at now: a clear, moderate, centre-left political party. This has itself not gone without internal criticism from the left of the party who believe that in modern years the party has become too moderate.

The ideological tensions inside the SNP are further complicated by the arguments between gradualists and fundamentalists. In essence, gradualists seek to advance Scotland to independence through further devolution, in a 'step-by-step' strategy. They tend to be in the moderate -left grouping, although much of the 79 Group was gradualist in approach. However, this 79 Group gradualism was as much a reaction against the fundamentalists of the day, many of whom believed the SNP should not take a clear left or right position.

This grouping of "neo-fundamentalists" have their roots within the camp of the former high-profile Labour Party MP Jim Sillars who left Labour to form the short-lived Scottish Labour Party in the 1970s (it had no connection with the UK Labour Party or the current Scottish Labour group in the Scottish Parliament). Sillars eventually joined the SNP, winning the Govan, Glasgow, by-election in 1988 to become an SNP MP. He lost the Westminster seat at the 1992 general election and expressed his disappointment by calling the Scottish people 'Ninety minute patriots'.

European Free Alliance

The SNP retains close links with Plaid Cymru and MPs of both parties co-operate closely with each other. They work as a single group within the House of Commons, and were involved in joint campaigning during the 2005 General Election campaign. Both are in the European Free Alliance (EFA), which works with the European Green Party to form a grouping in the European Parliament: the Greens - European Free Alliance. Although there is no coalition in the Scottish Parliament (the SNP having run a minority government since May 2007) the Scottish Greens supported the appointment of the government under an agreement which also specified areas of common policy and gave the Greens input to the budget process and convenorship of the parliamentary committee on transport, infrastructure and climate change.

Ministers and spokespeople

Scottish Parliament

See also: Government of the 3rd Scottish Parliament, Scottish Government, Members of the 3rd Scottish Parliament

Councillors

The SNP has more than 360 councillors in Local Government elected from the Scottish local elections, 2007.

Criticism

Accusations of anglophobia

The SNP have been charged with being "Anglophobic". In 2000, the Labour party said that two SNP members of the Scottish Parliament were anti-English after they "registered their support for Germany's (2006 Football World Cup) bid on its official website". The SNP responded that they "have no position on where the World Cup is held" and that it was "silly to describe the website entry as anti-English".

Prominent figures in Scottish politics such as Labour's George Foulkes, Baron Foulkes of Cumnock and the Liberal Democrats' Jamie Stone (and subsequently Danny Alexander - the current UK Government's Chief Secretary to the Treasury) have publicly apologised for calling the SNP "xenophobic". SNP MSP Ian McKee has by contrast pointed out his own status in the Scottish Parliament chamber as an Englishman as evidence of there being no such anti-English feeling. Indeed, McKee is one of six SNP MSPs born in England, along with other prominent figures such as Christine Grahame and Cabinet Secretary for Education and Lifelong Learning Mike Russell.

Accusations of "cash for policies"

The party has been criticised over a £500,000 donation from the transport businessman Brian Souter. One month later, in April 2007, the SNP's commitment (made at the party's 2006 conference) to re-regulate the bus network was not included in their 2007 manifesto, although the SNP denies any direct link. Opposition politicians suggested that the donation and policy shift were linked and that it was a case of "cash for policies", although no official accusations have been made.

Brian Souter went on to make a further donation of £125,000 to the SNP, making him their single biggest donor. Souter made approaches to the SNP government for a £3 million subsidy for his company, Stagecoach, to develop a hovercraft service between Kirkcaldy and Portobello in Scotland. The service had already received subsidy from the previous Labour administration for the pilot scheme, but was put on hold pending "clarification" of the public sector's involvement.

Source (edited): "http://en.wikipedia.org/wiki/Scottish_National_Party"

Scottish Party

The **Scottish Party** was formed in 1930 by a group of members of the Unionist Party who favoured the establishment of a Dominion Scottish Parliament within the British Empire and Commonwealth. They differed with the existing National Party of Scotland (NPS) on the grounds that their Scottish independence was ambiguous about the Empire, and also disagreed with the left-of-centre platform of the NPS.

The Scottish Party initially acted more as a think-tank than an active political party, but received overtures from the founder of the NPS, John MacCormick, to merge with the NPS to unify the elements of the Scottish independence movement. The party's candidate for the November 1933 by-election in Kilmarnock received NPS backing, and this co-operation concluded with the merger of the two parties in 1932 to become the Scottish National Party.

A minor, though unrelated, political party of the same name was founded in 2004 by a former member of the Scottish National Party, and changed its name to the Free Scotland Party shortly thereafter.

Source (edited): "http://en.wikipedia.org/wiki/Scottish_Party"

Scottish Socialist Party (1987)

The **Scottish Socialist Party** was a small political party operating in Scotland. It was primarily a left-wing breakaway from the Scottish National Party (SNP) although it succeeded in recruiting a number of Labour Party members, including the former Labour Group leader in Edinburgh council, Alex Wood. A group of dissident Labour Party and SNP members formed the Scottish Socialist Movement in 1987, shortly after the general election held that year and in 1988 the SMM became the Scottish Socialist Party.

It favoured the establishment of a Scottish socialist republic, independent of the United Kingdom.

The party contested only one parliamentary seat, Glasgow Central at the 1989 by-election, when its candidate Bill Kidd received 137 votes (0.5%). The party folded the following year and many of its members subsequently returned to the SNP, including Bill Kidd.

The party published a regular magazine, *Socialist Scotland* and had links with the Welsh socialist party, Cymru Goch.

This party is in no way related to the Scottish Socialist Party established in 1998.

Source (edited): "http://en.wikipedia.org/wiki/Scottish_Socialist_Party_(1987)"

The Scots Independent

The Scots Independent is a monthly Scottish political newspaper that is in favour of Scottish independence. It was formed in 1926 with William Gillies as editor, by the Scots National League (SNL) and switched its allegiance to the National Party of Scotland (NPS) when the SNL joined with them in 1928.

When the NPS merged with the Scottish Party in 1934 to form the Scottish National Party (SNP) they switched to supporting them. The paper is still today largely pro-SNP.

Published in Stirling, it currently has a circulation of around 6,000 and is read by supporters of Scots independence throughout the world.

It carries articles in Lowland Scots and Scottish Gaelic.

Source (edited): "http://en.wikipedia.org/wiki/The_Scots_Independent"

Young Scots for Independence

Young Scots for Independence (YSI) (Sometimes termed **SNP Youth**) is the youth wing of the Scottish National Party (SNP). It is not to be confused with Federation of Student Nationalists, which is for those in higher education, and whose membership is not restricted by age, unlike the YSI.

The YSI is autonomous from the SNP and as such is entitled to formulate its own policies and devise its own campaigns. The YSI is represented on the SNP National Executive Committee and can send delegates to meetings of the SNP Annual National Conference.

Objectives

Its objectives are:
- independence for Scotland;
- the furtherance of all Scottish interests;
- to increase support for the aims and policies of the SNP amongst the youth of Scotland;
- to provide a political and social forum for the youth of Scotland;
- to further the interests of the youth of Scotland;
- to campaign against the continued presence of nuclear weapons in Scotland and the wider world.

History

The YSI is a youth organisation set up to campaign for Scottish independence through the Scottish National Party (SNP). It is independent of, though affiliated to, the SNP. Formed in the 1970s as the **Young Scottish Nationalists** the organisation changed its name to YSI in 1996 when the YSN underwent a complete reorganisation.

Many YSI activists have since risen to prominence in the SNP, including Nicola Sturgeon the Deputy First Minister of Scotland, former party leader John Swinney, the Cabinet Secretary for Finance and Sustainable Growth and Fiona Hyslop, the Cabinet Secretary for Education and Lifelong Learning.

Text referendum

On 8 April 2006, the YSI launched a "text referendum" at the SNP Conference in Dundee, which asks people to vote via text message "Scot yes" or Scot no" on the question "should Scotland be independent?".

A text referendum on nuclear weapons was also launched, which asks people to vote on whether they believe the Westminster Government should spend £25 billion on a new generation of nuclear missiles to be stored on the River Clyde - 30 miles from Glasgow.

Speaking at the launch, the then YSI National Convenor Aileen Campbell said: "I am really excited about this referendum. It will allow us to truly engage with young people across Scotland and give them an opportunity to express their views using modern every day technology. The Electoral Commission wants parties to take proactive steps to engage with young voters and not just use them as publicity stunts. So we are taking the initiative and are asking the young people of Scotland to make their views known about Scotland's constitutional future!"

National Executive Committee

- **National Convener:** David Linden
- **Senior Vice Convener:** Alan Masterton
- **NationalSecretary:** Alex MacLeod
- **National Treasurer:** Michael Dixon
- **National Director of Publicity:** Kenny Murray
- **Under 18's Rep:** Austin Sheridan
- **National Organiser:** Janie Orr
- **Membership Secretary:** Conor McKay
- **YSI Rep to the FSN:** Ross Deans
- **Ordinary Executive Member:** TBC
- **Ordinary Executive Member:** TBC
- **Ordinary Executive Member:** TBC
- **YSI Rep to the SNP NEC:** David Linden

Branches

The YSI is split up into branches where there is a concentration of active members in a geographical area. Individual members who are not part of branches can, and do, become involved though participating on a more national scale.

The current branches are:
- Cumbernauld & Kilsyth
- Forth Valley
- Glasgow
- Highlands (including Moray)
- Lanarkshire
- Lewis and Harris
- Lothians
- Young Asian Scots for Independence

Source (edited): "http://en.wikipedia.org/wiki/Young_Scots_for_Independence"

Free Scotland Party

The **Free Scotland Party** is a minor political party in Scotland that stands for an independent Scotland, independent of both the United Kingdom and the European Union.

The party was founded by Brian Nugent, from Shetland, after he left the SNP due to disagreements over Europe. The party holds up Norway, a non-EU country, as an example for Scotland.

The party contested three constituencies in the 2005 general election campaigning on the issue of the fishing industry in Scotland. Maitland Kelly received 183 votes (0.4%) in Ochil and South Perthshire, Nugent received 176 votes (1.0%) in Orkney and Shetland, and Dallas Carter received 384 votes (1.0%) in Motherwell & Wishaw.

The party also stood in the Scottish Parliament election, 2007, gaining 664 votes (0.24%) in the Mid Scotland and Fife constituency. Jim Fairlie, a former deputy leader of the SNP and the party's finance spokesman, received 575 votes (1.65%) in Perth.

Source (edited): "http://en.wikipedia.org/wiki/Free_Scotland_Party"

Scottish Enterprise Party

The **Scottish Enterprise Party** (SEP) was a Scottish centre-right party supportive of Scottish independence. It was formed in July 2004 to provide an alternative for centrist and right-of-centre voters who support independence.

The party opposed Scottish membership of the European Union and any prospective membership of the euro; it supported the principle of a constitutional monarchy and elections conducted through the Single Transferable Vote.

The SEP took the constitutional view that, unlike in England where sovereignty traditionally resides with Parliament, in Scotland sovereignty constitutionally resides with the people, as set out in the Declaration of Arbroath.

The party fielded 3 candidates in the 2007 Scottish Parliamentary elections, obtaining a total of 1,025 votes.

The organisation was later renamed as the Scottish Democratic Alliance (SDA). The policies remained basically the same. The SDA was registered with the Electoral Commission in June 2009, and the SEP was simultaneously wound up.

Source (edited): "http://en.wikipedia.org/wiki/Scottish_Enterprise_Party"

Scottish Jacobite Party

The **Scottish Jacobite Party** is registered as a political party with the UK Electoral Commission.

Formed on 8 July 2005, it favoured the establishment of an independent Scottish republic based on the concept of a "unifying political theory" that "the citizen is king". This ideology states that if political decisions are made with this idea being consistently taken into account then temporary political expediency can be avoided and the public interest served. The notion that the people are central to the political process and their explicit support for republicanism does not fit with the traditional meaning of Jacobites - that is, those who favour the restoration of the House of Stuart to the Scottish (and indeed, English) monarchy. It stated its views to be a modern interpretation of Jacobitism.

It stated its aim as to establish their vision of a Scottish republic by 2007 which would, on independence claim 31% of the assets of the British State (as Scotland makes up 31% of the landmass of Britain).

Some of its other views included moving the Scottish and English border southwards to run from Morecambe Bay to Flamborough Head along latitude 54 degrees, 7 minutes North (thus adding Carlisle, Durham, Sunderland, Teesside and Tyneside to Scotland). In consequence, Newcastle United F.C., Sunderland A.F.C., Middlesbrough F.C. and Carlisle United F.C. would be transferred into the Scottish Premier League, It advocated that all football teams in this league should be nationalised, with television revenues being split equally amongst all participating clubs. Foreign players would also be banned from playing in Scotland.

Another policy was to transform Scotland into a tax haven and make it a more popular tourist destination, although it has also stated that congestion charges will be introduced at peak tourist season.

The party was registered with the Electoral Commission between 2005 and 2007. Its designated leader and treasurer is, or was, John Black, and its campaigns officer John Brodie.

In the 2007 Scottish elections, it nominated one candidate, John Black, who won 309 votes for the Dumbarton constituency, and 446 votes in the West of Scotland region. Its total expenditure was returned as £528, the lowest of any party to submit a return. It has filed an e-petition calling for a Scottish independence day.

The Jacobite Standard was raised above Glenfinnan by the Party, 260 years after Bonnie Prince Charlie did so in 1745.

The Scottish Jacobite Party was de-registered and removed from the Electoral Commission's Register of Political Parties on 19 July 2007.

The party was re-registered with The Electoral Commission on 22nd March 2010. John Black received 156 votes for this party in the 2010 election in Argyll and Bute. Chris Black polled 134 votes in Berwickshire, Roxburgh and Selkirk.

Source (edited): "http://en.wikipedia.org/wiki/Scottish_Jacobite_Party"

Scottish Republican Socialist Party

Glencoe commemoration

The **Scottish Republican Socialist Party (SRSP)** was a political party operating in Scotland. They were formed out of the **Scottish Republican Socialist Clubs**, formed in 1973 to introduce socialism to the Scottish National Party (SNP) and grow support for Scottish independence amongst left-wingers who supported the retention of the Union with the rest of the United Kingdom. The expulsion of the 79 Group from the SNP led to the Republican Clubs deciding to form as a coherent political party and they formed themselves into the SRSP in 1982.

Whilst agreeing with the SNP, insofar as they believed in independence, the SRSP believed that this should be combined with support for socialism. They argued that independence for the working class is meaningless unless it is socialist, and adopted an abstentionist position towards Westminster elections.

The SRSM has been active, not only campaigning for Scottish independence via the Independence First initiative, but by its Annual 1320 Declaration of Arbroath Rallies, Annual Glencoe Rallies, John MacLean commemoration and campaigning at a grassroots level.

SRSM & SSP

In 1998, the Scottish Socialist Party (SSP) was formed and the SRSP narrowly decided to join them, and re-formed as a cross-party movement called the **Scottish Republican Socialist Movement**. Many members ended up within the SSP, but not exclusively. In 2005, the SNP proscribed membership of the SRSM, claiming it was "SSP".

The SRSM was active in campaigning against attempts within the SSP to ditch the policy of supporting independence. It succeeded at persuading high profile SSP members like Alan McCombes, Rosie Kane and Kevin Williamson to speak at its rallies and for its cause.

In October 2006, the SRSM announced that it was disaffiliating with the Scottish Socialist Party and becoming a cross party organisation.

Magazine

The SRSM publishes a biannual magazine called *Scottish Worker's Republic*, a magazine called *Red Duster*. and a website.

Source (edited): "http://en.wikipedia.org/wiki/Scottish_Republican_Socialist_Party"

Scottish Socialist Party

The **Scottish Socialist Party (SSP)** (Scottish Gaelic: *Pàrtaidh Sòisealach na h-Alba*; Scots: *Scots Socialist Pairty*) is a left-wing Scottish political party. Positioning itself significantly to the left of Scotland's centre-left parties, the SSP campaigns on a socialist economic platform and for Scottish independence.

It operates through a branch-based structure with additional networks for identity or campaigning groups, as well as accepting open platforms who are allowed to organise within the party.

Following the 2003 elections to the Scottish Parliament, it had six Members of the Scottish Parliament (MSPs) and two local councillors, the SSP lost all its seats in the Scottish Parliament in the 2007 election and retained only one local councillor. In the 2011 Holyrood elections, the SSP is standing in all regional lists.

Its primary campaigns at the moment are centred around the cuts to public services being introduced by the UK government, demands for the establishment of an independent Scottish republic as well as the provision of free school meals.

History

The Scottish Socialist Party was formed from the Scottish Socialist Alliance (SSA), an alliance of left-wing organisations in Scotland, Following reasonable results by the alliance in the 1997 General Election, the decision was taken to transform the SSA from an electoral alliance into a single party to contest the first elections of the new Scottish Parliament. The SSP polled unexpectedly well in this election and saw the then National Convenor Tommy Sheridan elected to represent Glasgow.

The period following that election saw sustained growth for the SSP, including a boost to membership when the Socialist Workers Party in Scotland joined the SSP, and the Scottish section of the National Union of Rail, Maritime and Transport Workers affiliated to the party. During this period of sustained and rapid growth it recruited extensively from former members of the Labour Party and the Scottish National Party, in addition to trade unionists, environmentalists, and community campaigners.

The 2003 elections to the Scottish Parliament saw the SSP gain five additional seats across Scotland, becoming the largest left-wing party in Scottish politics.

On 11 November 2004 Tommy Sheridan announced his resignation as convener of the party, citing personal reasons, although it later emerged that he had effectively been recalled by the National Executive of the party. He was replaced by Colin Fox, SSP MSP for the Lothians, after a contest with Alan McCombes, the SSP's policy co-ordinator.

On 29 August 2006, Tommy Sheridan announced his intention to leave the Scottish Socialist Party and found a new socialist political party called Solidarity. The split was formalised in September 2006.

The SSP stood on the regional lists for the 2007 election, where it lost all remaining seats, and in council elections across the country, where it won just a single seat, Jim Bollan's in West Dunbartonshire. The party (12.450 votes; 0,6%) failed to gain as many votes as Tommy Sheridan's breakaway party, Solidarity.

However in 2008 it recovered to some extent, increasing its vote compared to 2007 and outpolling Solidarity in two by-elections in Glasgow East and Glenrothes. In 2009 the SSP was seriously involved in the Glasgow school closures protest, and it contested the 2009 European elections, largely around the slogan of 'Make Greed History', campaigning for a Europe wide 'greed tax' on the continent's rich, and marginally increased its vote compared to 2007.

The party ran ten candidates in the United Kingdom general election, 2010. All lost their deposits.

The SSP has decided to contest all eight regions in the Scottish Parliament election, 2011, with gender balanced lists of candidates. The no. 1 candidates are: West Jim Bollan, Glasgow Frances Curran, Central Kevin McVey, Lothian Colin Fox, South Colin Turbett, Mid Scotland and Fife Morag Balfour, North East Angela Gorrie, Highlands and Islands Pam Currie. These eight include two ex-MSPs as well as a sitting councillor a sitting councillor and demonstrates the party's commitment to representative diversity on the basis of gender, sexuality and disability.

Campaigns

Scottish Independence

The SSP strongly supports autonomy for Scotland and Scottish independence from the United Kingdom.

It co-ordinated the rally for independence at Calton Hill in October 2004 and wrote the Declaration of Calton Hill, which sets out a vision of an inclusive and outward looking Scottish republic, based on the key principles of liberty, equality, diversity and solidarity. A follow up event to mark the initial declaration was held in October 2005.

It also supports the Independence First campaign which demands an immediate referendum on independence for Scotland. In 2006, it participated in the "Rally for Independence" together with the other political parties who campaign for independence as part of a broad-based campaign to demand the right of self-determination for Scotland.

The national self-determination sought by the SSP is driven by internationalist rather than nationalist concerns. It seeks to build an inclusive republican state which is run by and for the benefit of all who live in Scotland. As such, it supports the rights of asylum seekers to settle there, without fear of detention or deportation; opposes the expansion of the UK state, for example through ID cards; and seeks the abolition of the monarchy.

Through prioritising independence as a key component in its political philosophy, it stands in the tradition of John Maclean who set up the Scottish Workers Republican Party in the early part of the 20th century, combining socialist economics with Scottish independence policies.

Reform of local government taxation

The Scottish Socialist Party claims to be at the forefront of the campaign to reform local government taxation.

Prior to the establishment of the SSP, a number of SSP members were subject to warrant sales after refusing to pay the Poll Tax. One of the first bills that the SSP put forward once elected to Holyrood became the Abolition of Poindings and Warrant Sales Act 2001, a popular action, which transformed debt recovery systems in Scotland.

The SSP propose a Scottish Service Tax, a form of local income tax to replace the current Council Tax, brought in after the Poll Tax became non-viable. A bill proposing a progressive local income based taxation was presented in 2005, however it was overwhelmingly defeated. The two other parties in the Scottish Parliament who support income based taxation, the Scottish Liberal Democrats and the Scottish National Party, disagreed with the proposals which would have seen anyone with an income below £10K pa exempted and anyone earning below £30K have their liability reduced, while targeting revenue generation to those with household incomes in excess of £100K.

Free prescription charges

In 2005, Colin Fox MSP proposed a bill to abolish prescription charges similar to that which allows Welsh citizens free prescriptions on the NHS. Despite widespread support and success at committee stage, it failed to become law.

In response to the bill and the publicity that it generated, the Scottish Executive announced a review of the impact that the charges had on the chronically sick and full time students just three hours prior to the bill being debated. This move was seen as a means of warding off the popular support that the campaign was receiving. The Scottish National Party announced the abolition of prescription charges since their last general election campaign. They are now abolished in Scotland. As a sop to the building pressure they also reduced the cost of prescriptions and extended the criteria for exemption.

From 1st April 2011, prescription charges were abolished in Scotland as a result of the pressure brought by the SSP.

Free school meals

Frances Curran, then an MSP, led a broad campaign with through many children's and anti-poverty organisations to provide free and nutritious meals for all Scottish schoolchildren to tackle the problems of poor diet and rising obesity amongst children.

This claimed to be able to eradicate the stigma associated with the current means tested system and also ensure that meals provided in school conformed to minimal nutritional standards.

A bill to this effect was proposed in parliament in 2002 but was defeated, however there is an increasing awareness of the role of diet on children's health and a subsequent Scottish Executive consultation found that 96% of respondents were in favour of free school meals.

A redrafted bill was launched in October 2006 and was resubmitted to the parliament. However, in November 2006 it was announced that this bill would not be taken in that session of parliament due to time pressures. Frances Curran had pledged that the SSP would resubmit its bill early in the next session of parliament and announced a text service for supporters to text Jack McConnell to demonstrate their support for the free school meals bill. However, the SSP's exit from parliament at the 2007 election prevented this.

Under pressure from the SSP and the wider campaign, the Scottish National Party (SNP) introduced free school meals as a pilot scheme for a small number of primary school pupils in selected local authorities and have announced that there will be free school meals for Primary 1-3 children from 2010, however have not backed the wholesale change that the SSP proposed.

Free public transport

The SSP has proposed the scrapping of all fares on public transport within Scotland, which they claim will reduce carbon emissions, cut road deaths, reduce air pollution and boost the incomes of workers reliant on public transport. The capital costs involved in the project would, they say, be raised by reducing planned roadbuilding programmes, in particular the M74 motorway extension, which the SSP has been active in opposing.

Such a scheme has a precedent in Hasselt, Belgium, where the city centre was revived by the provision of free public transport, and was a key plank of the Greater London Council's policy platform in the early 1980s.

Fuck Abstinence

Fuck Abstinence is a Scottish Socialist Youth Women's Group campaign that seeks to educate young women denied adequate sex education through the distribution of information on reproductive rights and to campaign for guarantees of such education in schools.

Reform of drug laws

The party has proposed the legalisation of cannabis and the licensing of premises to sell cannabis. It has also proposed the provision of free synthetic heroin on the National Health Service, under medical supervision to combat the problems of drugs in working class communities, as well as calling for a massive expansion in residential rehabilitation and detoxification facilities for addicts.

Anti-war campaigns

The SSP has campaigned against the Iraq War. The SSP was one of the founding members of the Scottish Coalition for Justice not War at its establishment in September 2001. The February 2003 march in Glasgow was attended by some SSP members, and later that year SSP MSPs were threatened with disciplinary action after SSP's Kevin Williamson staged a protest in the Scottish Parliament. In 2004, STV and Grampian threatened to pull a party political broadcast by the SSP which accused Tony Blair over the pretext for the war.

It works closely with Military Families Against the War, particularly in the Justice 4 Gordon Gentle campaign, standing down in the 2005 general election for Rose Gentle in the East Kilbride constituency.

It has also campaigned against rendition flights, including introducing a debate in the Scottish Parliament over the issue, and against the lack of response from the UK government in Israel's war on Lebanon.

It has supported the non-violent direct action as a tactic to oppose the presence of Weapons of Mass Destruction in Scotland and strongly opposes the replacement of Trident. It has participated in the blockades at Faslane nuclear base since its inception and a number of SSP members have been fined and/or jailed after blockading the naval base at the annual Big Blockade. In 2005, Rosie Kane locked herself on to a 25 foot Trident replica outside the Scottish Parliament, only releasing herself after the replica was dismantled 14 hours later. Later that year she was fined £150 for her actions and in October 2006, she was jailed for 14 days after refusing to pay the fine. In January 2007, three of its MSPs were arrested, later released without charge, while in June 2007, five members of the SSP's youth wing were also arrested and held overnight, after blockading the base as part of the Faslane365 campaign.

Make capitalism history

The party was highly active in the protests against the G8, joining the Make Poverty History march in Edinburgh and participating in the G8 Alternatives Summit.

Platforms

The party (unlike most others) allows for the organisation of internal factions (which it describes as platforms), the intention is to ensure that socialists can work together on the issues on which they agree, however to respect the opinions of other socialists on the issues on which there is dispute.

Current platforms

- The **Republican Communist Network** (born 1999) was a founding member of the SSP. It prints an internal journal *Emancipation and Liberation*.
- The **Workers Unity Platform** (born 1999) is an amalgam of members from small left groups who came together to form a platform within the SSP.
- The **Solidarity Tendency** (born 2006) consists of supporters of the Alliance for Workers Liberty.

Former platforms

Two of the former platforms in the SSP both emerged from British Section of the Committee for a Workers International, following the "Open Turn" debate of the early 1990s, which was largely led by Scottish members. In 1998, the "Scottish Debate" led to the establishment of the SSP, however within the UK movement this was not widely welcomed. Tensions between many leading Scottish members, including Alan McCombes and Catriona Grant, and the UK leadership led to a split within the CWI into two separate platforms. The SWP joined in 2003 following extensive negotiations between the leaderships of the two parties, leaving in 2006 to join Solidarity. The United Left platform was formed in early 2006 in the midst of the internal problems which eventually led to the split in the party, after which the platform formally dissolved.

- The **International Socialist Movement** (1999–2006) was a founder member of the SSP and was affiliated to the CWI. It broke from the CWI in 2001, when some CWI loyalists left it. It published the journal "Frontline" until its dissolution in 2006, whereupon Frontline became an independent Marxist journal.
- The **International Socialists** (2001–2006) consisted of a small number of individuals who remained affiliated to the CWI when the ISM broke away from the international in 2001. In 2006 the platform left the party.
- The **Scottish Republican Socialist Movement** (1999–2006) whose major focus is independence for a Scottish Republic, emerged from the Scottish Republican Socialist Party which was one of the founding platforms of the SSP. The SRSM officially disaffiliated from the SSP in November 2006, although some individual members remain SSP members.
- The Scottish supporters of the **Socialist Workers Party** (2003–2006) joined the SSP in 2002 becoming the Socialist Workers Platform despite strong reservations from then members. In 2006 they left the SSP to join Solidarity.
- The **United Left** (2006–2007) was not officially incorporated as a platform within the SSP, however it operated in a similar manner and was largely regarded as such. It was formed in June 2006 and dissolved in January 2007. Its formation was largely in response to the Sheridan crisis however it drove a move towards a more collaborative and autonomous vision for the SSP in the post-split period.

SSP's role in the Sheridan trials

Tommy Sheridan sued the *News of the World* for defamation when, immediately following his controversial resignation, it was alleged that he had had an extra marital affair. As a result of his lawsuit the minutes of the SSP executive meeting held on 9 November 2004 were subpoenaed by the newspaper. The party initially declined to hand them over. A raid was conducted on the SSP's offices in May 2006 and Alan McCombes, the SSP's national policy co-ordinator (who had possession of them) was jailed for 12 days. In response to a call from Sheridan to release the minutes, the party eventually handed them in to the court. It transpired that in that meeting the party executive had decided, unanimously, to ask for his resignation because he intended to take the *News of the World* to court for defamation over allegations that were in fact true.

Sheridan claimed in the press that a cabal within the party's Executive Committee were out to destroy him, and expanded on this statement in an open letter to party members on 28 May 2006, claiming there had been a long-standing slander campaign conducted against him by senior party figures and MSPs.

At his court case eleven SSP members testified that Sheridan admitted during the 9 November meeting to having attended a swingers' club, an admission which is noted in the disputed minutes, repeated to Charlie McCarthy and five other leading members in the SSP, as well as recorded on a videotape which surfaced in October 2006. However, this video tape has been disputed by Sheridan that it was faked using excerpts of his voice to piece it together. Sheridan eventually won his court case though an appeal has been lodged on behalf of the *News of the World*. A police investigation into allegations of perjury, conspiracy to commit perjury and witness intimidation has followed the trial. Computers from both the SSP and Sheridan's Parliamentary offices were seized for forensic examination. On 1 April 2007, *The Sunday Herald* reported that Lothian and Borders Police had reached a conclusion about the disputed minute. On 16 December 2007, Sheridan was charged with perjury related to the case.

The trial of Tommy and Gail Sheridan started at Glasgow High Court on 4 October 2010 and a number of SSP members were called as witnesses. In December 2010, Tommy Sheridan was found guilty of perjury. His wife Gail was acquitted.

Criticism

The Socialist Workers Party have criticised the SSP for no longer being a broad and open mass party of the left, and cited this as one of their reasons for splitting from the SSP to form Solidarity. The SWP and others on the left have also argued that the SSP has not responded adequately to wide public anger at recent wars. However, SSP defenders have contested that these opinions are based around the Socialist Workers Party's pre- 2007 support for Sheridan's ally and maverick left-wing Respect party politician, George Galloway, who has been at odds with the SSP leadership over issues like independence, amongst others.

Other information

The SSP distributes a weekly newspaper, the *Scottish Socialist Voice*.

The SSP is a founding member of the European Anticapitalist Left.

The SSP has an active youth wing, Scottish Socialist Youth.

The SSP has an active women's net-

work, the Socialist Women's Network
    SSP members helped establish Second Life Left Unity

Local Government representation

SSP local councillors

- Jim Bollan (West Dunbartonshire Council)

Holyrood representation

1999 elections

The SSP contested the 1999 Scottish elections in all of the eight regions. One member was elected in the Glasgow region.

2003 elections

The SSP contested the 2003 Scottish elections in all of the eight regions and most first past the post seats gaining 245,735 votes in total (4.7%). Six representatives were elected to the Scottish parliament from the regional lists including two in Glasgow, one in Central, one in Lothians and one in South of Scotland. In 2006, two of these representatives left the party, leaving the SSP with four MSPs.

2007 elections

The SSP contested the 2007 Scottish elections in all of the eight regions. It won 12,731 votes across the eight regional lists, less than 10% of its results in 2003. It failed to gain any seats and lost all four of its MSPs.

Source (edited): "http://en.wikipedia.org/wiki/Scottish_Socialist_Party"